# TABLE & FLOOR

### easy to make - fun to play

# GAMES

# TABLE & FLOOR

### easy to make - fun to play

# GAMES

## By:

## Liz & Dick Wilmes

A BUILDING BLOCKS Publication

## ART

| | |
|---|---|
| Cover Direction: | David VanDelinder<br>STUDIO 155<br>Elgin, Illinois 60123 |
| Text Illustration: | David Jensen<br>DAVID JENSEN DESIGN<br>Elgin, Illinois, 60123 |
| Cover Design, Game and Pattern Art: | Nel Gammon Webster |
| Typesetting and Layout Mechanicals: | Greg Wilmes<br>David Jensen |

## SPECIAL THANKS TO

Karen Burt, Vohny Moehling, and Dawn Zavodsky for helping us design and refine the games included in MAKE-TAKE GAMES.

Early childhood librarians at Gail Borden Library in Elgin,IL for sharing their "Off To School" game.

Authors of Channels To Children for inspiring the "Whiskers Says" game.

Margie Robertson for sharing "Dress Frosty".

PUBLISHED BY:
BUILDING BLOCKS
38W567 Brindlewood
Elgin, Illinois 60123

DISTRIBUTED BY:
GRYPHON HOUSE
P.O. Box 275
Mt. Rainier, MD 20712

ISBN 0-943452-16-3
$ 16.95

**DEDICATED TO:**

...caring adults who nurture young children.

# Contents

## SPRING GAMES

## SUMMER GAMES

## PATTERNS

# TIPS AND TECHNIQUES

When Making A Game Remember To:

~ Take your time.

~ Read the directions first.

~ Decide if you want to vary your game and how.

~ Gather all of your materials and supplies before you begin.

~ Use materials from your scrap box when possible.

~ Cut slowly and slant into the board, paper, or fabric
   which you are cutting.

~ Lay out your game before you glue it down.  Make
   adjustments if needed.

~ Use a minimal amount of glue, especially if you are going
   to laminate your game and pieces.

~ Let the glue dry before laminating.

~ Leave an edge of laminate or Contact® paper when trimming.

~ Save your patterns.

~ Make pockets for all of your game pieces:
   -- Attach them to the back of game boards.
   -- Resealable plastic bags hooked to the game board with a
       metal ring.
   -- Small plastic containers.
   -- Coffee cans.

~ Have a "Missing Piece Box" in your room, so that when
   children find game pieces they can easily save them.

# When Gathering Supplies and Materials Think About:

**~ Markers**
-- Use permanent markers to draw your lines.
-- Use watercolor markers to color your game pieces, cards and boards.
-- Have wide-tipped and fine-tipped available.

**~ Glue**
-- Waterdown your white glue.
-- Brush on your glue so that it is smooth.
-- Use a non-aerosol spray glue instead of white glue.
-- Use fabric glue when making felt board games.
-- Use a minimal amount of glue especially when laminating or using Contact .

**~ Colored Paper**
-- Use a heavier weight paper from an art supply store. The colors are truer and brighter than regular construction paper.

**~ Scissors**
-- Use sharp scissors.
-- Cut slowly.
-- Cut into your paper or board for smooth edges and sharper corners.

**~ X-Acto Knives**
-- Be safe.
-- Slit your pieces carefully and slowly, so that you only cut what is necessary.

# OFF TO SCHOOL

**(Use Pattern Pages 147-150)**

## YOU'LL NEED

4 pieces of yellow construction paper
Several pieces of construction paper
Set of colored markers/crayons
Permanent black marker
16" magnetic tape
Clear Contact® paper/laminating if available

## TO MAKE <u>OFF TO SCHOOL</u>

**Game Buses**

1. Cut 4, 5"x10" rectangles from the yellow construction paper.

2. Trace a simple school bus shape on each one. Cut each out.

3. With permanent marker, write a numeral (1-4) in the middle of each bus.

4. Add detail to each bus.

**Game Children**

1. Cut 15, 3"x6" rectangles from construction paper.

2. Duplicate and color all of the children and glue them to the construction paper.

3. Write a numeral (1-4) on each shirt. Cut out the children.

**Protect Your Game**

1. Laminate the game or cover both sides of each Bus and Child with clear Contact® paper.

2. Cut 8, inch pieces from your magnetic tape. Glue 2 pieces to each bus. Cut 15, half inch pieces from your magnetic tape. Glue one piece to each child.

3. Store the game in a large resealable plastic bag. Attach a metal ring to it and hang in your classroom.

## TO PLAY <u>OFF TO SCHOOL</u>

1. Take the buses and children out of the bag. Put the 4 buses on a magnetic board and the 15 children on the floor or table.

2. Pick up one child, look at the numeral on his shirt and put him on the magnetic board near his school bus. Pick up another child and help him board his bus.

3. Continue until all of the children are "off to school".

*While Playing Talk About*
~ Bus safety.
~ What the players see inside a real bus.
~ Bus rides the players might have taken.
~ Things the players like to do at school.

# TO VARY YOUR GAME

♦ **SHAPE MATCH:** Instead of writing numerals 1-4 on the buses and children, choose 4 shapes. Draw a big shape on each bus. Add a shape to each child's shirt.

To play, help the children get on the right bus by matching the shapes.

♦♦ **DOT MATCH:** Instead of writing the numerals 1-4 on the buses and children, draw dots representing the number values on them.

♦♦♦ **BOARD YOUR BUS:** When constructing the game, make 4 buses and write the numerals 1-4 on them. Make 10 children. On one child's shirt write the number 1, on 2 other children the numeral 2, on 3 more children the numeral 3, and on the last 4 children the numeral 4.

To play, match the numerals on the children's clothes with their buses. To make this even more difficult, do not write numerals on the children's clothes, simply ask the players to put the right number of children on each bus.

13

# IN THE APPLE TREE

(Use Pattern Page 151)

## YOU'LL NEED

1 piece of corrugated cardboard from a large grocery box or packing box
1 piece of green posterboard
1 piece of dark brown or black posterboard
1 piece of red posterboard
1 piece of tan or light brown construction paper
White glue

## TO MAKE <u>IN THE APPLE TREE</u>

**Game Board**

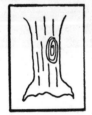

1. Cut a 16"x28" rectangle from your piece of corrugated cardboard.

2. Cut a 14"x16" rectangle from your piece of green posterboard.

3. Draw a bushy tree on the green posterboard and then cut it out.

4. Cut a 5"x8" rectangle from your dark posterboard.

5. Draw a trunk on the dark posterboard and then cut it out.

6. Glue the tree and trunk to the piece of corrugated cardboard.

**Game Pieces**

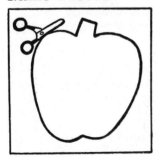

1. Cut 9, 3"x3" squares from your red posterboard.

2. Trace an apple on each of the squares and cut them out.

3. Cut each apple in half using a different pattern.

4. Glue half of each apple to the apple tree.

14

**Storage Pocket**

1. Cut a 4"x6" rectangle from your piece of tan construction paper.

2. Trace a bushel basket on it. Cut it out. Add details.

3. Carefully brush glue along the sides and bottom half of the bushel basket and glue it next to the tree. The top half of the basket should be left unglued.

4. Slip the other half of each apple into the basket.

## TO PLAY <u>IN THE APPLE TREE</u>

1. Take the apple halves out of the bushel basket.

2. Lay the pieces near the tree.

3. Fit the halves together to make big, juicy red apples.

*While Playing Talk About*
- ~ Eating apples.
- ~ Picking apples.
- ~ Different colors of apples.
- ~ Times the players may have made applesauce.
- ~ How many apples are on the tree puzzle.

16

# TO VARY YOUR GAME

♦ **MATCH THE APPLES:** Change the object of the game. Instead of pairing apple halves, draw 7-8 different size apples on the red posterboard. Cut them. Trace and cut out a second set of red apples. Glue one set on the tree. To play match the second set of apples to those hanging on the tree.

♦ **SIMPLE PUZZLES:** Make the cuts in your apples very simple and thus easier to match.

♦♦ **FRUIT TREES:** Construct additional fruit tree puzzles such as orange, pear, banana, coconut, and cherry trees.

♦♦♦ **LARGE APPLE PUZZLES:** Construct individual apple puzzles. Cut several large apples. Cut each apple into 3 or more pieces. (You might want to code the backs of each apple piece or cut different colored apples so they are self-correcting.) To play, lay all of the pieces on a tray and put the puzzles together.

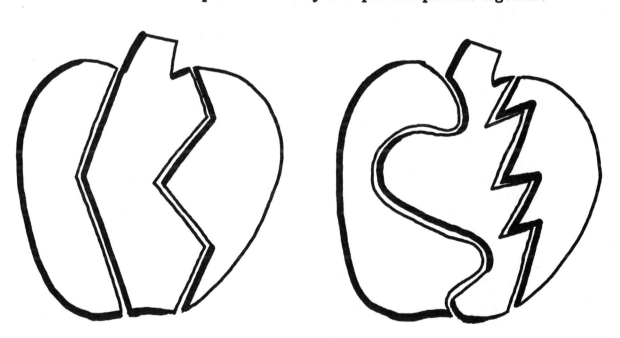

# SHAPE MATCH

(Use Pattern Pages 152-159)

## YOU'LL NEED

1 piece of colored posterboard
3-4 pieces of white construction paper
1 piece of black construction paper
1 piece of lightweight cardboard/tagboard
Colored markers or crayons
Permanent black marker
1 metal brad
Clear Contact® paper/laminating if available

## TO MAKE SHAPE MATCH

**Game Board**

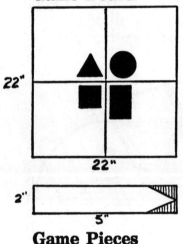

1. Divide the black construction paper into 4 equal sections. Trace one shape in each section and then cut it out.

2. Cut the piece of posterboard into a 22"x22" square. With a permanent black marker divide the piece of posterboard into 4 equal squares. Glue one black shape in each of the 4 middle corners of the board.

3. Cut a 2"x5" rectangle from the extra piece of posterboard. Make it into a spinner by cutting one end into a point.

**Game Pieces**

1. Duplicate and color all of the objects and glue them to construction paper.

2. Color the pictures.

3. Cut out each picture.

18

19

**Storage Pocket**

1. Cut a 6"x9" rectangle from the piece of lightweight cardboard.

2. Round the bottom corners to look like a pocket. Add detail.

3. Drizzle glue along the 2 sides and bottom edge of the pocket and fasten it to the back of the game board.

**Protect Your Game**

1. Laminate the game or cover both sides of the Game Board, Spinner, and Game Pieces with clear Contact® paper.

2. Attach the spinner to the center of the board with the brad.

3. Carefully slit open the top edge of your storage pocket.

4. Store the game pieces in the pocket.

## TO PLAY <u>SHAPE MATCH</u>

1. Take the game pieces out of the storage pocket and lay them near the board.

2. Look at the shapes in the center of the game board.

3. Flick the spinner. Look at the shape it stops on.

4. Decide which game piece reminds you of that shape. Lay the piece near the black shape. Flick the spinner again and add a second picture to the board. Continue until all of the pieces are on the game board. (Remember, this is a judgement-type game. Players need only to have a reason why they chose each match.)

### *While Playing Talk About*
~ The names of the shapes on the game board.
~ The different shapes you see in the game pieces.
~ Reasons for making each match.
~ Shapes the players might see in their clothes.

# TO VARY THE GAME

♦ **ONE SHAPE ONLY:** Construct the game so that the pictures on the game pieces accent only one shape.

♦ **TWO SHAPES ONLY:** Divide the game board in half and feature only 2 shapes and less pieces.

♦ **BLOCK MATCH:** Instead of using the pictures, get a variety of different shapes blocks and match them to the shapes on the game board.

♦♦♦ **MORE SHAPES:** Construct the game board using more difficult shapes such as an oval, star, hexagon, semi-circle, and/or diamond. Add appropriate game pictures.

♦♦♦ **OBJECT MATCH:** Instead of using the pictures, gather a variety of objects, put them in a basket, and match the shapes in the objects to the shapes on the game board.

# DINO JUMP

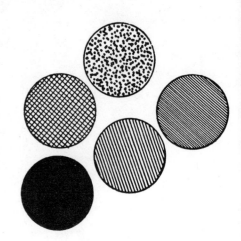

## YOU'LL NEED

1 sheet of colored posterboard
1 piece of white lightweight paper, such as ditto paper
15, 1¼" self-adhesive round dots in 5 different colors
1 set of markers to match the 5 colored dots
1 metal brad
White glue
Black permanent marker
Clear Contact® paper/laminating if available

## TO MAKE DINO JUMP

**Game Board**

1. Draw a very simple dinosaur shape on the piece of posterboard. Cut out the dinosaur.

2. Add the trail of colored dots and dino prints along Dino's back. Be sure to mix up the colors.

3. To make the color wheel, cut out a 6" to 7" circle from the lightweight paper. Divide it into 6 equal sections. Color each section to match one of the colored dots. Draw a dino print in the sixth section. Glue the circle to the center of the dinosaur.

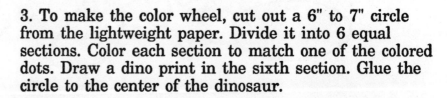

4. To make the spinner cut a 2"x5" rectangle out of the white posterboard. Draw a dinosaur bone on it. Cut it out and draw an arrow down the middle.

5. Add details to your dinosaur.

start

23

**Protect Your Game**    1. Laminate the game or cover both sides of the Dinosaur and Spinner with clear Contact® paper.

2. Loosely attach the spinner to the middle of the color wheel with a brad.

## TO PLAY <u>DINO JUMP</u>

1. Get movers for each player. Colored blocks or plastic mini dinosaurs work well.

2. Have the first player flick the spinner. When the spinner stops, name the color.  That player walks his mover along Dino's back, stopping at the matching color. Each player flicks the spinner and moves along Dino's back in the same manner. If a player lands on a colored dino print, stop and clap for the player.

3. Continue until everyone has walked down Dino's back to the end of his tail.

*While Playing Talk About*
~ Dinosaurs.
~ Colors.
~ Whether the players would like to play "Dino Jump" with their families.

# TO VARY YOUR GAME

♦ **CREATE A DINO STORY:** Instead of putting a trail of colored dots along Dino's back, draw a trail of Dino prints. Give each player a mover. Tell the players that they are going to join Dino on an imaginary walk through the Dinosaur Grocery Store.

Have the first player slowly walk his mover from one print to the next until you say, "Stop." The player lays his mover on that print. Say, "What does Dino see at the grocery store?" (Discuss.) Continue in this manner stopping along the way until everyone has walked to the end and is checking out their groceries.

Next time you play take a walk through other places such as the zoo, park, fire station, etc.

♦♦ **BACKWARDS DINO JUMP:** Play the game backwards, walking up Dino's tail and along his back.

♦♦ **COLOR DINO JUMP:** Give each player a mover. Have the first player name a color and put his mover on it. Continue until everyone's movers are on Dino's back. Now have the first player name another color and move his markers to a dot or dino print of that color. Continue until the players have landed on the last space.

♦♦♦ **NUMBER DINO JUMP:** When constructing the game divide the wheel by numbers (1-4) instead of colors. When you play, flick the spinner, name the numeral that it points to, and then walk your mover that many places.

# WALK AROUND THE ZOO

(Use Pattern Pages 160-166)

## YOU'LL NEED

Gray, white, yellow, brown, and green felt or construction paper
Black and brown permanent markers
Felt board
Large resealable plastic bag

## TO MAKE <u>WALK AROUND THE ZOO</u>

**Zoo Animals**

1. On the appropriate colors of felt or construction paper draw a simple elephant, zebra, giraffe, monkey, snake, lion, tiger, kangaroo, camel, and hippopotamus. (You could simply duplicate and color the zoo animal patterns.)

2. Using markers add details to each animal.

3. Cut out the animals.

4. If you make your animals out of paper, back each one with a large piece of felt.

5. Duplicate the story, <u>Walk Around the Zoo.</u>

**Protect Your Game**

1. Laminate the story or cover both sides of it with clear Contact^R paper.

2. Store the zoo animals and the story in the resealable plastic bag.

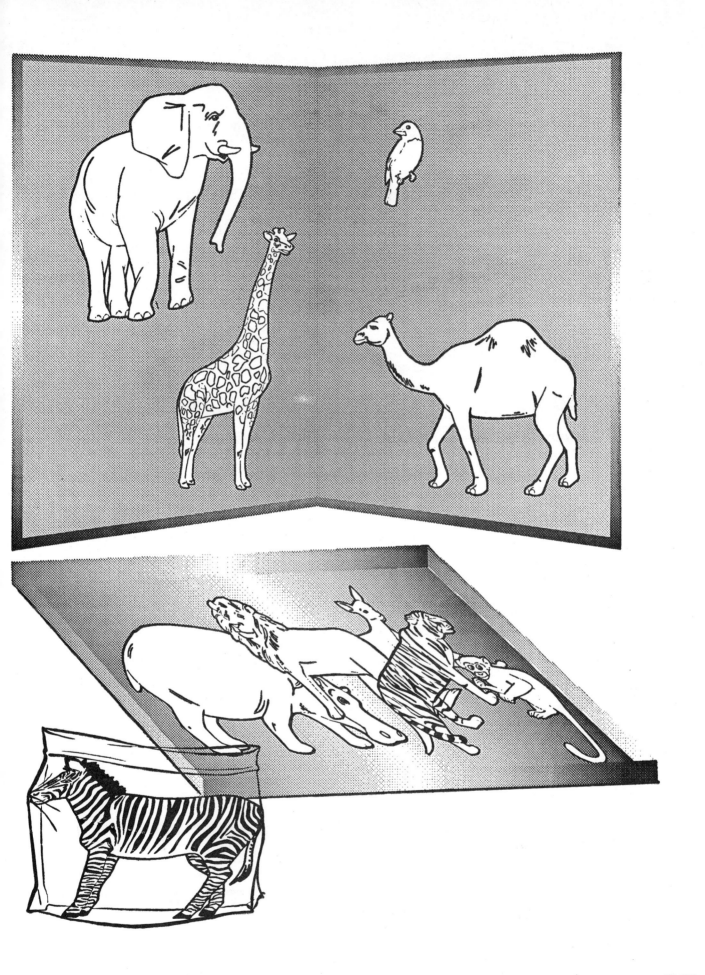

# TO PLAY <u>WALK AROUND THE ZOO</u>

1. Lay all of the animals on a tray or in a shallow gift box.

2. Set the animals near the felt board.

3. Begin to tell/read the story. When you get to the first animal riddle, let the children guess what animal you saw first. Put it on the felt board. Continue the story, letting the children put the animals on the board as you all continue your walk around the zoo.

**While Playing Talk About**
~ Children's trips to the zoo.
~ Animal pictures they've seen.
~ Noises each animal makes.
~ After the story enjoy saying some favorite zoo animal fingerplays.

## <u>YELLOW GIRAFFE</u>

*The yellow giraffe is tall as can be.*
*His lunch is a bunch of leaves off a tree.*
*He has a long neck and his legs are long too.*
*He runs faster than his friends at the zoo.*

## <u>ELEPHANT</u>

*Right foot, left foot, see me go.*
*I am gray and big and slow.*
*I come walking down the street,*
*With my trunk and four big feet.*

## <u>BROWN BEAR</u>

*Brown bear, brown bear turn around.*
*Brown bear, brown bear touch the ground.*

*Brown bear, brown bear walk along.*
*Brown bear, brown bear sing a song.*

## <u>BABY KANGAROO</u>

*Jump, jump, jump*
*Goes the big kangaroo.*
*I thought there was one,*
*But I now see two.*

*The mother takes her young ones*
*Along in a pouch,*
*Where they can nap,*
*Like children on a couch.*

*Jump, jump, jump*
*Goes the mother kangaroo.*
*Wherever she goes,*
*Her babies go too.*

# WALK AROUND THE ZOO

It was a bright, cool morning and our family decided to go to the zoo. We quickly packed a picnic lunch and were off for the day. We arrived at the gate just as the zoo was opening. As we walked in, there were several black and white striped animals running around in a field. What were the first animals we saw? LET THE CHILDREN ANSWER AND THEN PUT THAT ANIMAL ON THE FELT BOARD. THIS IS THE FORMAT FOR THE REST OF THE STORY.

Our family continued walking along the path. Soon we came to an animal that had a long gray trunk and a huge body. ELEPHANT We stood watching the elephant for awhile. We would have liked to throw him peanuts, but there was a sign that said, *"DO NOT FEED THE ELEPHANTS."*

We proceeded along watching many of the animals romping around. After awhile we came to one of my very favorite animals. This animal had a long neck, was yellow, and was covered with large brown spots. GIRAFFE We stood there for awhile watching the giraffe eat leaves from the top of a tall tree. Dad said, *"Let's be on our way. There are lots more animals to enjoy."*

He was right! The very next ones we saw made us laugh all the while we watched them. These animals played on trapezes, liked to swing from branches, tires, and ropes. They were? MONKEYS As with many of the other animals, we could have enjoyed the monkeys all day; however, it was getting close to lunchtime.

We sat on the picnic bench and ate. While we ate many birds flew around in the trees overhead. Well, lunch was over. We cleaned up and continued our walk around the zoo. CONTINUE THE STORY USING THE ZOO ANIMALS THAT YOUR CHILDREN CAN IDENTIFY. AFTER THREE OR FOUR MORE ANIMALS END THE STORY.

The sun was setting and we were all very tired. We agreed that it was about time to go home. We stopped to have a drink of water and then went to the car. The next thing I remember was that mom and dad were carrying my brother and I into the house.

*by Liz Wilmes*

# CLIP IT

### (Use Pattern Page 167)

## YOU'LL NEED

1 piece of white posterboard
1 piece of red, green, yellow, purple, brown, black, orange, and blue construction paper
1, 3"x7" piece of white posterboard
Yardstick
Permanent black marker
1 metal brad
Giant colored paper clips to match each piece of construction paper
Clear Contact® paper/laminating if available
1 resealable sandwich bag
Paper punch
Metal ring

## TO MAKE CLIP IT

### Color Wheel

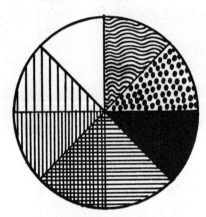

1. Cut a 17" circle from your piece of white posterboard.

2. Divide the circle into 8 equal sections.

3. Cut each piece of colored construction paper into a wedge that fits into one of the sections.

4. Glue the wedges to the sections.

5. Make the spinner by tracing a crayon shape on the 3"x7" rectangle. Cut it out. Add detail.

### Protect Your Game

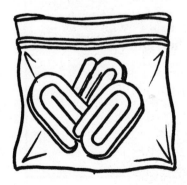

1. Laminate the game or cover both sides of the Color Wheel and Spinner with clear Contact® paper.

2. Attach the spinner to the center of the color wheel with the brad.

3. Store the giant paper clips in the plastic bag. You may want to punch a hole in the color wheel and bag and then clip the bag to the wheel with a metal ring.

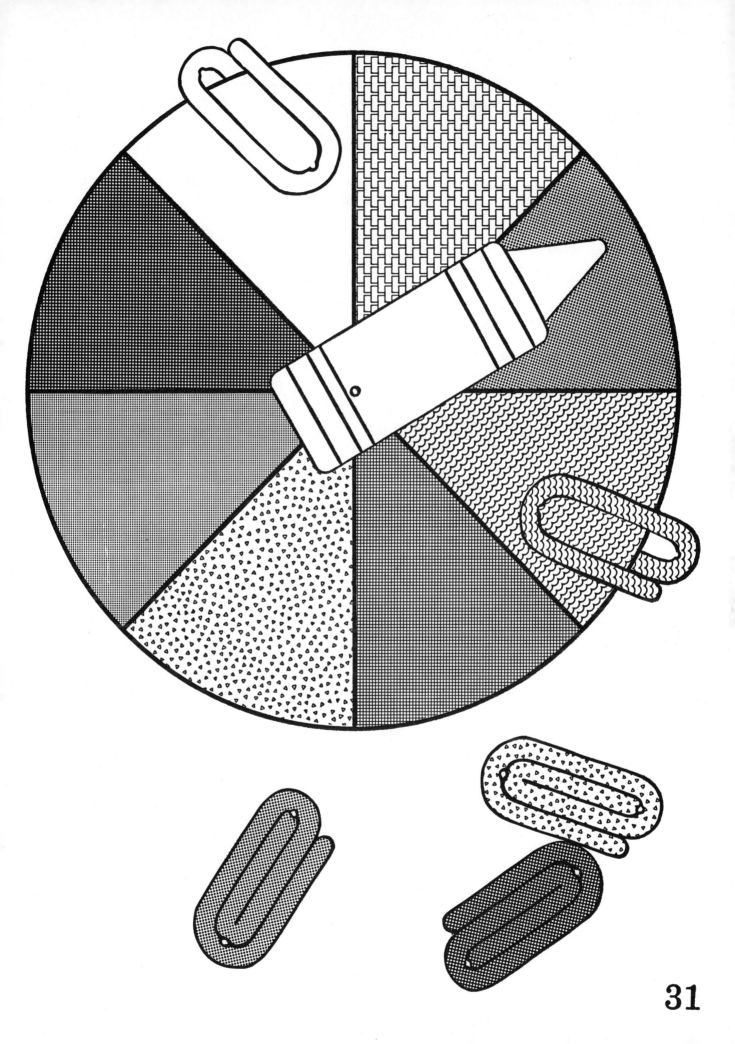

31

# TO PLAY <u>CLIP IT</u>

1. Lay the color wheel on the floor or table. Put the colored clips near it.

2. Flick the spinner. Look at the color which the spinner stopped on, find a matching clip, and slide it onto the wheel.

3. Continue until all of the clips are attached to the different sections of the wheel.

4. Reverse the game. Flick the spinner, let it stop, and slide a clip off of the color wheel and return it to the bag. Continue until all of the clips are off of the wheel.

*While Playing Talk About*
- ~ The colors on the color wheel.
- ~ Colors of the clips that match the player's clothes.
- ~ What players think the giant clips could be used for.
- ~ How to slide the clips onto the color wheel.

# TO VARY YOUR GAME

♦ **PARK THE CARS:** Instead of playing the game with clips, have a box of small colored cars. Flick the spinner. Look at the color which the spinner stopped on, find a matching car, drive it up to the section, and park it. Continue until all of the cars are parked.

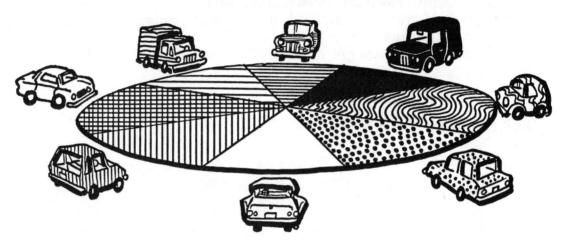

♦♦ **CLIP THE CLOTHESPINS:** Instead of clipping giant paper clips to the wheel, use different sizes of colored clothespins.

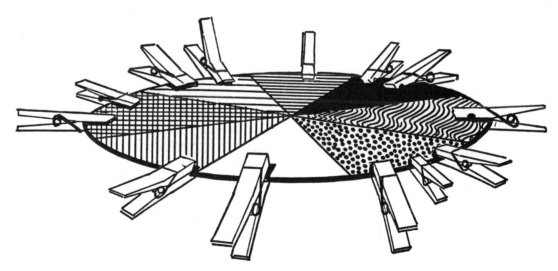

♦♦♦ **PASTEL CLIP IT:** Construct your color wheel using pastel colors instead of the 8 basic ones.

33

# RAKE THEM UP

(Use Pattern Pages 168-174)

## YOU'LL NEED

1 colored file folder
2 pieces of light brown/tan construction paper
1 piece each of green, yellow, red, purple, and orange construction paper
Permanent black marker
1 small piece of lightweight cardboard/tagboard
Clear Contact® paper/laminating if available

## TO MAKE RAKE THEM UP

**Game Board**

1. On the pieces of tan construction paper, trace a small, medium, and large bushel basket. Cut them out and add detail.

2. Open your file folder and turn it the long way.

3. Carefully brush glue along the sides and bottom half of the smallest bushel basket. Glue it in the top left hand area of the folder. Glue the mid-size basket in the top right area and the largest one in the middle of the bottom section.

**Game Cards**

1. Construct 5 sets of leaves for the game. First pick one type of leaf. Trace a small, medium, and large one on a sheet of construction paper. Then choose 4 other types of leaves and trace small, medium, and large ones on the other four colors of construction paper.

2. Add detail to the leaves and cut them out.

34

Rake Them Up

35

**Storage Pocket**

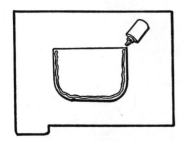

1. Cut a 4"x8" rectangle from the piece of lightweight cardboard.

2. Round the bottom corners to look like pockets. Add detail.

3. Drizzle glue along the sides and bottom edge of the pocket and fasten it to the back of the file folder.

**Front Cover**

1. Cut out several additional leaves and a rake. Glue them on the front cover.

2. Print the name of the game on the folder tab.

**Protect Your Game**

1. Laminate the game or cover both sides of the File Folder and Leaves with clear Contact® paper.

2. Carefully slit the top edge of your storage pocket and bushel baskets.

3. Store the leaves in your storage pocket.

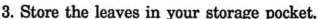
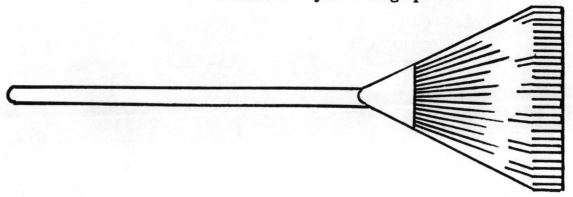

## TO PLAY <u>RAKE THEM UP</u>

1. Take the leaves out of the storage pocket. Open up the folder and lay the leaves near it.

2. Begin raking up the leaves by grouping them into 5 colors.

3. Take one set of leaves, find the smallest leaf and slip it into the smallest basket, slip the medium leaf into the medium basket, and the largest leaf into the largest basket. Rake the other sets of leaves up in the same way.

***While Playing Talk About***
~ Times the players have raked up real leaves.
~ Games to play in the leaves.
~ Colors of the fall leaves.
~ Leaves the players have found.

# TO VARY YOUR GAME

♦ **EASY RAKE UP:** When constructing the game, make only a large and small bushel basket and sets of large and small leaves.

♦♦ **COLORED LEAF RAKE UP:** When constructing your game, use only one type of leaf. Using the same small, medium, and large leaf patterns, make sets of leaves using different colors of construction paper.

   To play, sort the leaves by color and then rake them into the different size bushel baskets.

♦♦♦ **LOTS OF LEAVES:** When constructing the game, make four different size bushel baskets and four different size leaves in each set.

# ALPHABET CRASH

(Use Pattern Pages 175-176)

## YOU'LL NEED

1 piece of colored posterboard
6 pieces of white construction paper
Permanent black marker
2 different colored markers
1 piece of lightweight cardboard/tagboard
Clear Contact® paper/laminating if available

## TO MAKE <u>ALPHABET CRASH</u>

**Game Board**

1. Cut a 4½"x4" rectangle out of lightweight cardboard. Trace a 4"x3¾" garage shape on it and cut it out.

2. Trace 6 garages, equally spaced along the top edge of your piece of posterboard. Trace 3 more rows leaving ¾" between each one.

3. On the roofs of the first 22 garages print pairs of upper and lower case letters. On the last 2, print 2 pairs of letters each.

**Game Cards**

1. Draw 52, 2½"x3¼" rectangles on the 6 pieces of white construction paper.

2. Trace a simple 2"x3" car shape on the piece of lightweight cardboard. Cut it out.

3. On 26 rectangles trace cars facing to the right and print a capital letter on each one. On the remaining rectangles, trace 26 cars facing to the left and print a lower case letter on each one.

4. Color the tires of capital letter cars one color and lower case cars another color.

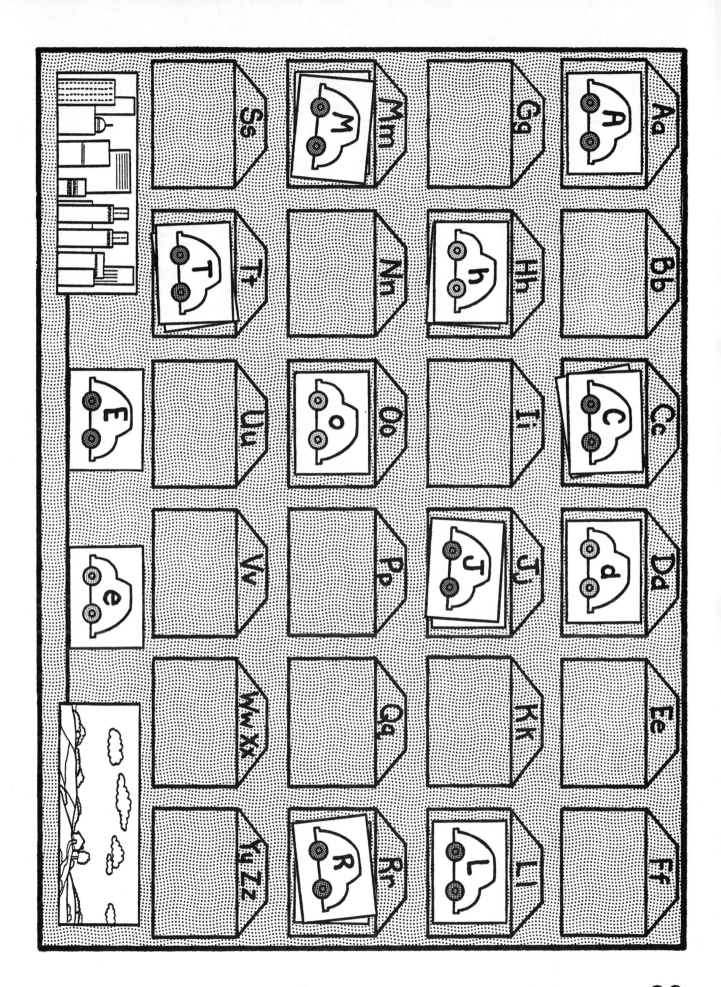

**Storage Pockets**

1. Cut 2, 3"x7" rectangles from lightweight cardboard. Duplicate and glue the skyscrapers on one pocket and the low buildings on the second pocket.

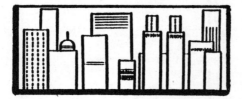 

2. Drizzle glue along the sides and bottom edges of the pockets. Fasten the pocket with the skyscrapers near the bottom left hand corner of the game board and the other pocket near the bottom right hand corner.

4. Connect the 2 pockets with a road.

**Protect Your Game**

1. Laminate the game or cover both sides of the Game Board and Game Cards with clear Contact® paper.

2. Carefully slit open the top edge of your 2 storage pockets.

3. Store the capital letters in the left pocket and the lower case letters in the right pocket.

## TO PLAY <u>ALPHABET CRASH</u>

1. Lay the cards face up next to each side of the board.

2. One player chooses a capital letter and lays it on the road. The other player chooses what he thinks is the matching lower case letter and lays it on the road.

3. The players drive down the road and crash along the way.

4. The players tow their cars to the appropriate garage and check the name of the garage to see if both of their cars belong there. If they do, the players leave their cars to be repaired. If not, they search for the right garages and leave the cars there.

5. Continue pairing cars until they are all being repaired.

*While Playing Talk About*
~ The names of the letters.
~ Which letters are in the players names.

40

## TO VARY YOUR GAME

♦ **EASIER CRASH:** When constructing the cards and the garages, use only upper case or lower case letters. To play, the players pair cars with identical letters and tow them to the garages for repair.

♦♦ **NAME THAT LETTER:** When construction the game board, simply draw 52, 2½"x3¼" rectangles on a piece of posterboard. Print an upper or lower case letter in each one.

When constructing the game cards, make 52 letter cards and 8 'Crash' cards, making 60 in all.

To play, have the players sit around the board. The leader has all of the cards. Hold up a card for the first player to see. Have that player name the letter on the card or you tell him what it is. The player takes the card and lays it in the appropriate rectangle on the game board. If you hold up a 'Crash' card, the player skips his turn. Continue until all of the cards have been named and are matched on the board.

♦♦♦ **ALPHABET CONCENTRATION:** Lay all of the game cards face down. The first player turns 2 cards over. If it's a match, the player keeps the cards; if not, he turns them back over. The second player turns 2 cards over and tries to make a match. If he does, he keeps the cards; if not, he turns them back over. Continue until all of the cards are paired.

# DRESS FROSTY

(Use Pattern Pages 177-178)

## YOU'LL NEED

2 pieces of white posterboard
Set of 8 colored markers
1 piece of lightweight cardboard/tagboard
1 metal brad
Clear Contact® paper/laminating if available

## TO MAKE <u>DRESS FROSTY</u>

**Frosty's Wheel**

1. Cut a 10" circle from your white posterboard. Divide it into 8 equal sections.

2. In each section trace different Frosty props, features or articles of clothing. (2 boots, broom, carrot nose, top hat, 2 buttons, scarf, 2 coal eyes, a smiling mouth) Color them with markers.

3. Make the spinner by drawing a broom shape on a 2"x6" rectangle. Cut it out.

**Game Boards**

1. Cut 4, 5"x9" rectangles from the white posterboard.

2. Trace simple snowmen shapes on the rectangles and then cut them out.

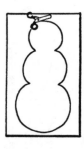

**Storage Pocket**

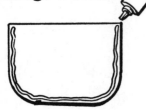

1. Cut a 3"x7" rectangle from lightweight cardboard. Round the bottom corners to make it look like a pocket.

2. Drizzle glue along the 2 sides and bottom edge of the pocket and fasten it to the back of Frosty's Wheel.

44

45

**Game Pieces**

1. Cut 32, 4"x4" squares from the piece of white posterboard.

2. Make 4 sets of the props, features, and articles of clothing to match the ones used on Frosty's Wheel. Color and cut them out.

**Protect Your Game**

1. Laminate the game or cover both sides of Frosty's Wheel, the spinner, and the 4 sets of Frosty and his Accessories with clear Contact® paper.

2. Carefully slit open the top edge of your storage pocket. Store Frosty's accessories in it.

3. Attach your spinner to center of Frosty's Wheel with the brad.

# TO PLAY DRESS FROSTY

1. Give each player a Frosty and a set of his accessories.

2. Put Frosty's Wheel in the middle.

3. Have the first player flick the spinner. When it stops, name the accessory. Have him find that piece and begin dressing his Frosty. (If the spinner stops on an accessory which has 2 pieces, such as the boots, the player adds only 1 piece per turn.) The second player flicks the spinner and begins dressing his Frosty in the same manner. Continue until each Frosty is completely dressed.

*While Playing Talk About*
~ The story of Frosty the Snowman. Listen to the song.
~ Times the players have built snow figures and buildings.
~ Other things the players do in the snow.
~ Clothes they wear outside in the snow.

**46**

# TO VARY THE GAME

♦ **DRESS FROSTY:** Do not use the spinner board. Let the first player name one of Frosty's accessories and then put it on his snowman. The second person names one of the accessories and begins dressing his Frosty. Continue in this manner until all of the Frostys are dressed.

♦♦ **COLORFUL FROSTY:** Instead of using Frosty's Wheel, use a color wheel. (See CLIP IT, page 30.) Flick the spinner and dress Frosty by matching the colors on the color wheel to Frosty's accessories.

♦♦♦ **GIANT FROSTY:** Instead of constructing a Frosty for each player, have one giant Frosty. Make facial features, clothes, and additional accessories to fit the bigger Frosty. Change Frosty's Wheel to match your pieces. Let the players flick the spinner and dress the giant Frosty.

# PETER PANDA JUGGLES COLORS

**(Use Pattern Pages 179-180)**

## YOU'LL NEED

1 piece of 12"x17" black felt
1 piece of 9"x12" white felt
1 piece each of 8 different colors of construction paper
1 piece of any color felt
Straight pins
White fabric glue
Permanent black marker
1 resealable sandwich bag
Clear Contact® paper/laminating if available

## TO MAKE <u>PETER PANDA</u>

**Peter Panda**

1. On a large sheet of white paper make 2 patterns for your panda. First trace and cut out a large basic panda shape. Next trace and cut out a pattern for the white part of your panda.

2. Pin the large basic panda shape to your piece of black felt and cut it out.

3. Pin the second pattern to your white felt and cut it out.

4. Lay the white felt in place over the black felt. Glue the pieces together.

5. Use the remaining felt for his eyes and nose.

6. Draw a mouth with your marker.

7. Cut a bow for your panda and glue it to his neck.

**Game Pieces**

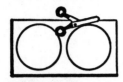

1. Cut a 3"x6" rectangle from each piece of construction paper.

2. Cut 2, 23/4" circles from each rectangle.

**Protect Your Game**

1. Laminate the colored circles or cover both sides of them with clear Contact® paper.

2. Glue small pieces of felt to the backs of the circles, so that they easily stick to the felt board.

3. Put Peter's colored circles in the resealable sandwich bag.

# TO PLAY <u>PETER PANDA</u>

1. Put Peter on the felt board.

2. Lay all of the colored circles near the board.

3. Pick up one colored circle and put it on the felt board. Look for its mate. When you find it, put it next to the first one.

4. Continue until all of Peter's colored circles are matched on the board.

*While Playing Talk About*
- ~ The names of the different colors that Peter is matching.
- ~ Colors the players are wearing. Do any of them match colors that Peter is juggling?
- ~ The players favorite colors.

# TO VARY YOUR GAME

♦ **BEGINNING COLORS:** Make fewer colored circles for Peter to match. You could make each circle a little larger.

♦♦ **PETER PANDA JUGGLES:** Let Peter juggle other things. He can match shapes, clothes, animals, letters, toys, foods, etc.

♦♦♦ **PETER PANDA STACKS HIS COLORS:** Draw and cut out a series of the same color circles only graduated in size from small to large. Make as many circles as you think your children can handle. Let Peter juggle them from smallest to largest or vice versa.

♦♦♦ **SORT THE SHAPES:** Peter can also categorize. For example put a variety of shapes of different colors near the board. To play help Peter find all of the triangles, or all of the purple shapes, or only the small shapes, and so on.

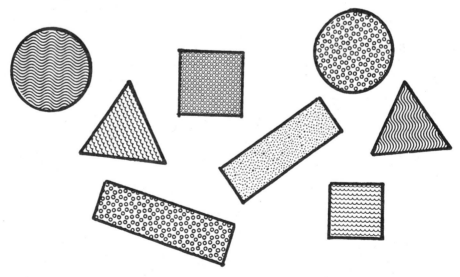

# SAMMY SHAPE

(Use Pattern Pages 181-183)

## YOU'LL NEED

2 pieces of white posterboard
1 set of colored markers
Large scrap pieces of colored posterboard to match your markers
Ruler
Permanent black marker
1 piece of lightweight cardboard/tagboard
Clear Contact® paper/laminating if available

## TO MAKE SAMMY SHAPE

**Game Pieces**

1. Using one piece of white posterboard, trace and cut out the following shapes:
  - 2, 2½" circles
  - 2, 2¾"x3¾" rectangles
  - 2, 3¾" squares
  - 1, 3¾"x3¾"x6" triangle
  - 1, 6" square
  - 2, 5"x5"x3½" triangles
  - 2, 1½" squares
  - 1, 5" square
  - 2, 3"x1" rectangles
  - 1, 4" square

2. Using the shapes that you just made, cut out a matching set of shapes from the different colored posterboard scraps.

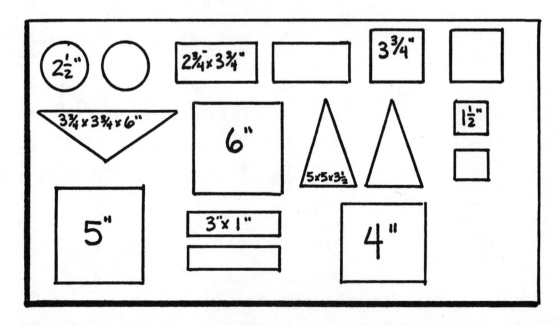

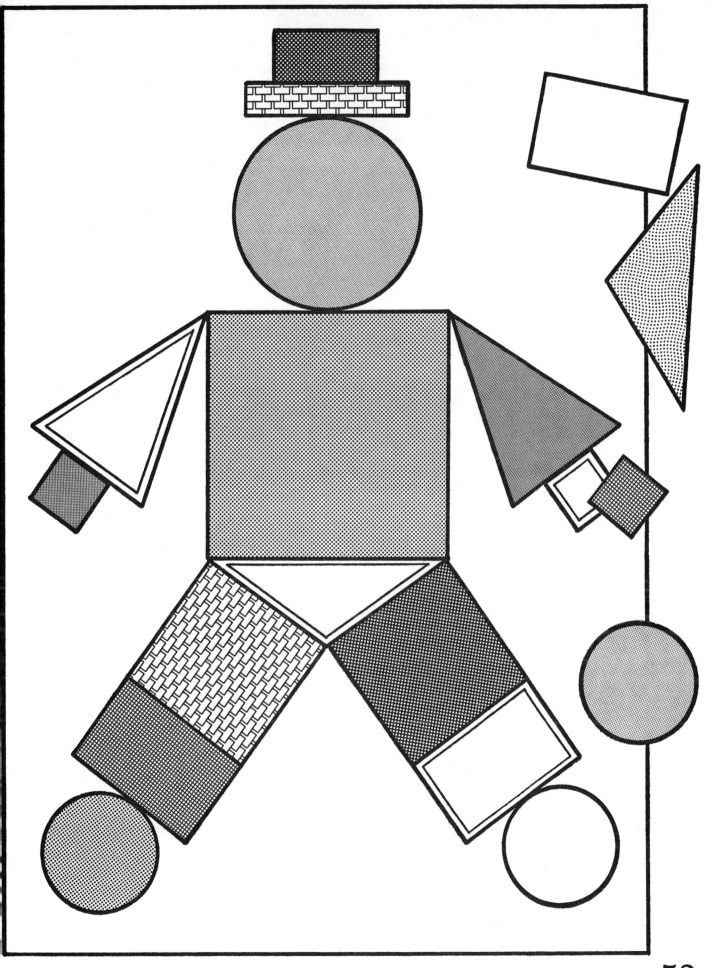

53

**Game Board**

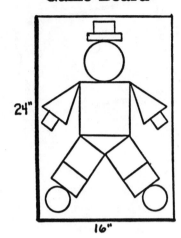

24"

16"

1. Cut a 16"x24" rectangle from the other piece of white posterboard.

2. Using the white shapes that you cut, layout your "Sammy Shape" on the rectangle.

3. After Sammy is laid out exactly the way you want, trace around all of the shapes with black marker, so that you have an exact duplicate of him.

4. Lay the colored posterboard shapes on Sammy. Using markers which match the color of each shape, outline each shape just inside of your black lines.

**Storage Pocket**

1. Cut a 6"x10" rectangle from the piece of lightweight cardboard. Round the edges to look like a pocket.

2. Drizzle glue along the sides and bottom edge of the pocket and fasten it to the back of Sammy.

**Protect Your Game**

1. Laminate the game or cover both sides of the Sammy Shape and the Individual Shapes with clear Contact® paper.

2. Carefully slit open the top edge of your storage pocket.

3. Store the individual shapes in the pocket.

# TO PLAY <u>SAMMY SHAPE</u>

1. Lay the individual colored shapes near Sammy.

2. Pick up one shape, find its mate on Sammy, and lay it down. Continue in the same manner until all of the shapes are matched and Sammy is full of color.

*While Playing Talk About*
   ~ The names of the shapes.
   ~ Shapes in the player's bodies, such as circle eyes and triangle noses.
   ~ What Sammy might be thinking about.

# TO VARY YOUR GAME

♦ **EASY SAMMY:** Make Sammy Shape with less pieces.

♦ **COLORFUL SAMMY:** When constructing Sammy, color in each of his shapes to match the colored pieces. For example if the matching square for Sammy's hat is black, color his shape black.

♦♦♦ **DRESS SAMMY:** When constructing the game, add a variety of additional pieces which are not drawn on Sammy Shape, so that when a player has finished matching all of Sammy, the player can add buttons, facial details, and other decorations he would like Sammy to have.

♦♦♦ **SAMMY PUZZLE:** Lay Sammy Shape on the table or floor. Instead of matching the shapes, use the pieces and construct another Sammy next to the board. Does Sammy have a twin now? What's his/her name?

# ALPHABET SOUP

(Use Pattern Page 184-185)

## YOU'LL NEED

3 lb metal coffee can with a plastic lid
1 piece of white posterboard
Permanent black marker
Piece of slightly patterned Contact® paper approximately 7½"x25"
14" of magnetic tape
White glue
Clear Contact® paper/laminating if available

## TO MAKE ALPHABET SOUP

**Game Can**

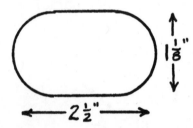

1. Trace a 1⅛"x2½" oval on your piece of posterboard. Cut it out.

2. Keeping the backing sheet fastened to the Contact® paper, wrap it around the can to make sure that it fits. Trim excess paper from the length, not the width, because it wraps over the top and inside of the can.

3. Lay your piece of Contact® paper, color side up, flat on a table. Using the oval pattern and a permanent marker, trace 26 ovals equally spaced on the paper.

4. On the left side of each oval, print (with permanent marker) an upper case letter, A-Z.

5. Carefully take the backing sheet off of the Contact® paper and wrap it around the coffee can. Wrap the excess paper over the top and inside of the can.

6. Cut out a circle from the excess Contact® paper to fit on the top of the plastic lid. Using your oval pattern, trace an oval and print "Alphabet Soup" on it. Fasten the circle on the lid of the can.

**Game Pieces**

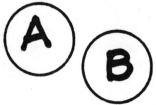

1. Cut a ⅞" circle from your piece of white posterboard.

2. Using the circle trace 26 circles. Print one upper case letter on each circle, A-Z. Cut them out.

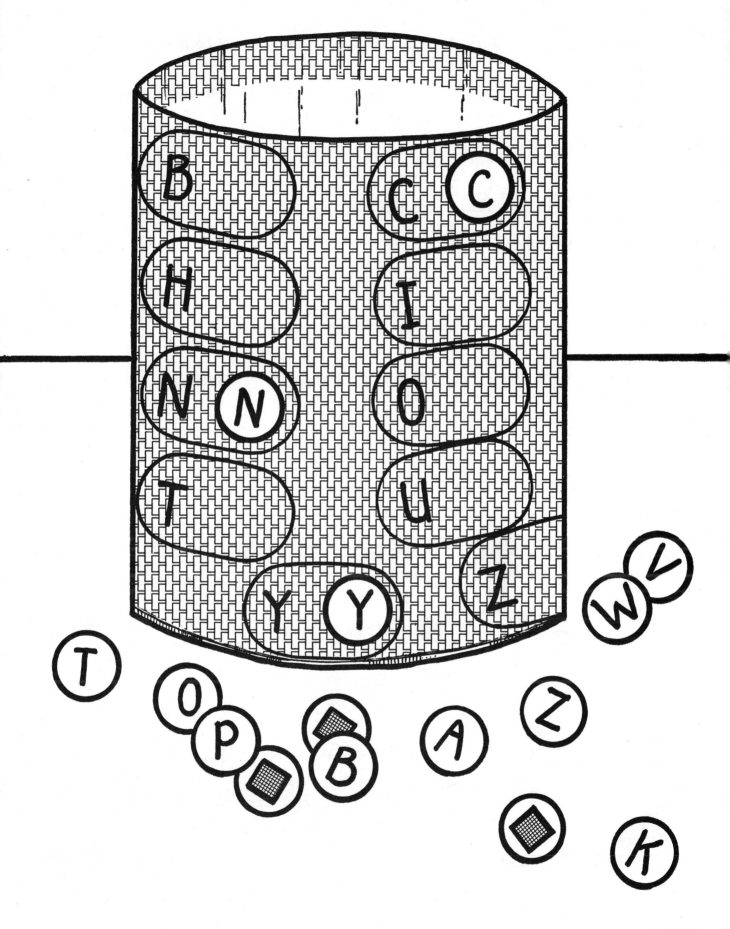

**Protect Your Game**

1. Laminate the letters or cover both sides of each one with clear Contact® paper.

2. Cut your magnetic tape into 26 equal pieces, about 1/2" each. Glue one piece to the back of each letter.

3. Store the letters inside the can.

## TO PLAY ALPHABET SOUP

1. Take all of the letters out of the can.

2. Pick up one letter, find its mate on the can, and place it inside of the oval.

3. Continue until all of the letters are matched.

*While Playing Talk About*
~ The names of the letters which the players are matching.
~ Letters which the players see in the room.
~ The players favorite stories.

# TO VARY YOUR GAME

♦ **LETTER RECOGNITION:** When constructing the game can, trace 26 ovals on the Contact[R] paper. Don't print anything in them. Wrap the Contact[R] paper around the can. Trace 26 ovals on white posterboard. On each oval print a letter, A-Z, a-z, or pair of letters, Aa-Zz. To Play: Put a Letter inside each oval on the can.

♦♦ **LOWER CASE MATCH:** Make the game so that players can match lower case letters instead of upper case ones.

♦♦♦ **PAIR THE LETTERS:** When constructing the game, print upper case letters on the ovals on the game can and the lower case letters on the games pieces. To Play: Pair the upper and lower case letters.

♦♦♦ **LETTER SOUNDS:** When constructing the game can, print lower case letters in each oval. Draw pictures on each game piece to correspond with the beginning sound of each letter. To play, match the letters with the pictures or the pictures with the letters.

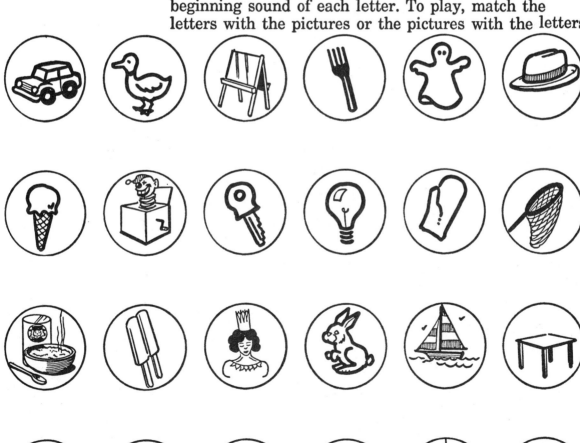

59

# NUMBER FLIP

## YOU'LL NEED

1 piece of colored posterboard
1 piece of white posterboard
55, 1" smiley stickers
4 metal rings
Permanent black marker
Paper punch
Clear Contact® paper/laminating if available

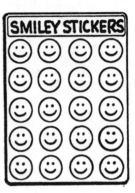

## TO MAKE <u>NUMBER FLIP</u>

**Front/Back Cover**

1. Cut 2, 7"x9" rectangles from your piece of colored posterboard. One will be the front cover and the other one will be the back cover.

2. On the front cover piece print, "Number Flip" in big letters. Write the numerals 1-10 on the rest of the cover.

3. Leave the back cover blank.

**Book Pages**

1. Cut 20, 4"x7" rectangles from your piece of white posterboard.

2. Divide the 20 rectangles into 2 piles of 10 each.

3. On one set, write the numerals 1-10 near the center of each page.

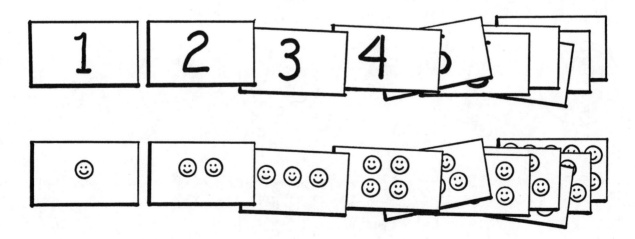

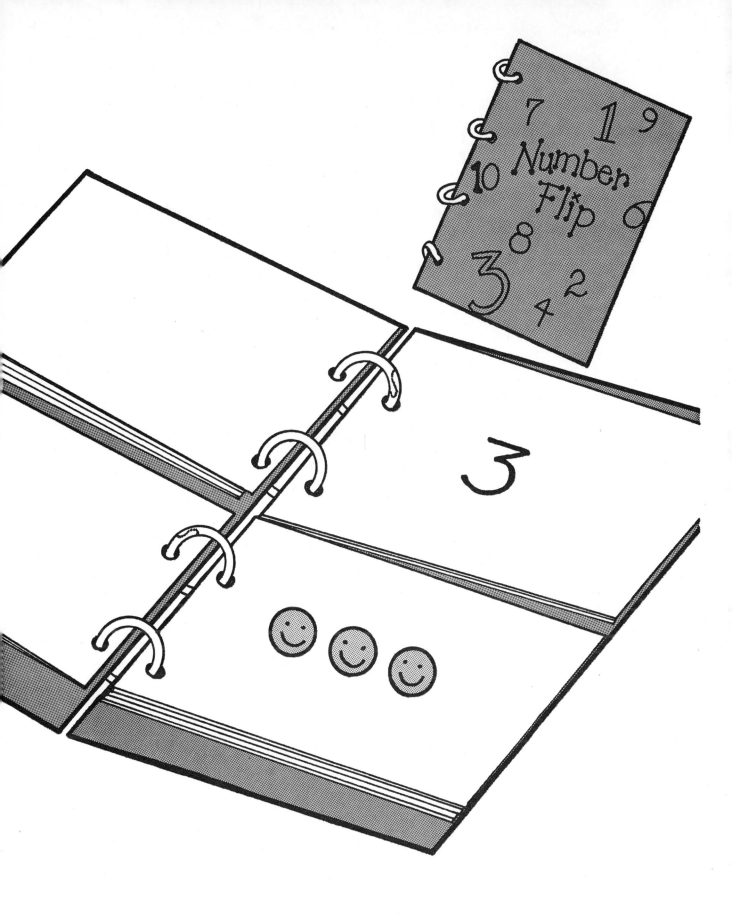

4. On the second set, put the smiley stickers on in groups of 1-10.

5. Arrange the pages with the numerals on them in order.

6. Mix-up the pages with the stickers on them.

7. Assemble the book, so that the numerals are on top and the stickers are on the bottom.

8. Punch 2 holes through the front cover, numeral pages and back page. Repeat for the sticker pages.

**Protect Your Book**

1. Laminate the book or cover both sides of the Front and Back Cover and all of the Pages with clear Contact® paper.

2. Re-punch the holes and clip the book together with the 4 metal rings.

## TO PLAY <u>NUMBER FLIP</u>

1. Open the book and look at the first numeral.

2. Flip the pages of "smiley stickers" until you find the page with one sticker on it. Count the sticker to double check.

3. Turn to the second page with numeral 2 written on it. Find the page with 2 stickers on it. Count them.

4. Continue until you have found all of the smiley faces.

*While Playing Talk About*
~ Counting.
~ What each numeral looks like.
~ What the different smiley stickers might be thinking about or why they are feeling happy.
~ What makes the players happy.

## TO VARY YOUR GAME

♦ **COUNT THE DOTS:** When making the top pages, put dot/s about the size of a dime above each numeral.

♦♦ **FIND THE NUMERAL:** Instead of looking at the numeral and finding the matching set of stickers, begin by counting the number of stickers and then finding the corresponding numeral.

♦♦♦ **READING NUMBER WORDS:** When making the top pages, print the number word rather than numeral on each page. You could add a dot/s above each word if you wish.

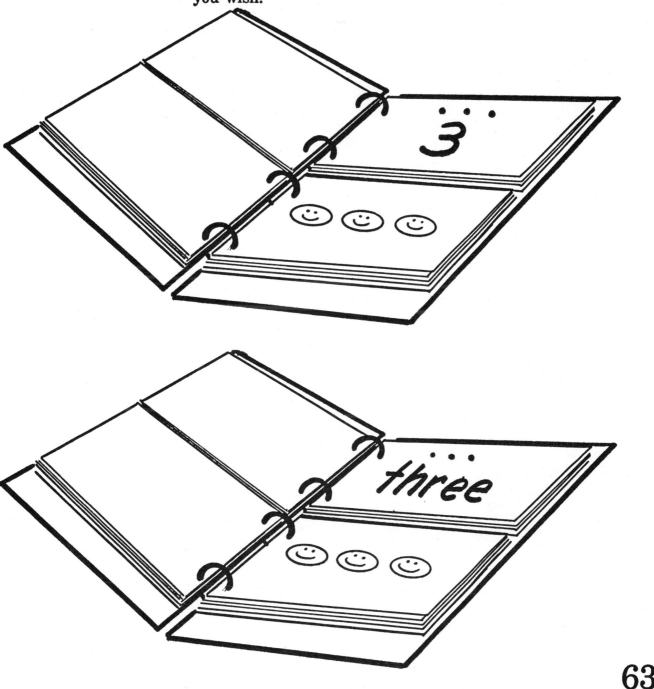

# GREGORY GROUNDHOG

**(Use Pattern Pages 186-191)**

## YOU'LL NEED

3 pieces of black construction paper
7-8 pieces of a variety of colors of construction paper
10 popsicle sticks or tongue depressors
Permanent black markers
White glue
Clear Contact® paper/laminating if available
Copy of the story
1 pocket folder

## TO MAKE <u>GREGORY GROUNDHOG LOOKS FOR HIS SHADOW</u>

**Puppets**

1. On different colors of construction paper, trace a very simple deer, rabbit, squirrel, bear, snake, bird, turtle, and groundhog. Cut out each animal and add details. (You could also duplicate and color each animal pattern.)

2. Lay each animal face up on the black construction paper. Draw an outline around it. Cut out the animal's shadow.

**Protect Your Game**

1. Cover the front side of the animal and the back of his shadow with clear Contact® paper.

2. Glue the popsicle stick/tongue depressor between the animal and his shadow.

3. Laminate a copy of the story or cover both sides of it with clear Contact® paper.

4. Store the puppets and a copy of the story in a pocket folder.

Gregory
Groundhog

# TO PLAY <u>GREGORY GROUNDHOG</u>

1. Lay all of the stick puppets down so that the shadows are face up.

2. Hold up Gregory Groundhog so that the listeners can see him. Begin reading/telling the story. When you get to the shadow which Gregory sees first, hold up the shadow of the bear. Hold Gregory and the bear's shadow next to each other. Talk about who the shadow could be and why. Turn the shadow around and see what animal Gregory really saw first.

3. Continue reading/telling the story, looking at and discussing the different shadows, and identifying Gregory's forest animal friends.

***While Playing Talk About***
- ~ Animals the children have seen and what they were doing.
- ~ The way different animals move.
- ~ Where in the forest different animals live, such as a bird in a nest, the turtle near the pond, squirrel in a tree, bear in a cave, and so on.
- ~ Sounds that the animals make.
- ~ What Gregory will do back in his burrow.

# GREGORY GROUNDHOG LOOKS FOR HIS SHADOW

Gregory had been sleeping in his burrow for several months. He felt it was time to get up and look for his shadow. Gregory slowly came out of his burrow. He stretched and yawned and then started looking around. First, he saw a shadow that was so big he knew it could not be his. WHAT DO YOU THINK GREGORY SAW? It was a huge _bear_. Gregory kept walking until he noticed another shadow in front of him. This one had wings. Gregory looked down at himself. He didn't have wings. LET THE LISTENERS GUESS. "I know," he said to himself, "It must be a _bird_."

He continued on through the forest. There were several more friends. Their shadows had long, fluffy tails. Gregory's tail was short. TALK ABOUT WHAT ANIMALS THESE MIGHT BE AND WHY. They were _squirrels_, having a wonderful time chasing up, down, and all around the trees.

Gregory thought that it was very strange that he was seeing everyone's shadow but his own. "I'd better try a little harder," he said to himself. With a smile on his face, he started walking. Soon he came to a pond. He thought maybe he would see his shadow reflecting in the water. But no, it wasn't there. The first thing that he saw was a moving shadow taking giant leaps from rock to rock. "What could that be?" Gregory wondered. It stopped moving and he instantly recognized it. WHAT DO YOU THINK GREGORY SAW? It was a _frog_. He laughed to himself as he moved on.

As he was walking along the bank, he noticed another moving shadow. This one moved very slowly, not quickly like the frog. He thought for a minute. TALK ABOUT WHICH OF GREGORY'S FRIENDS THIS WAS. Then he remembered that this animal was called a _turtle_. And speaking of slow moving friends, there went a long, skinny friend slipping through the grass. WHAT ANIMAL WOULD SLITHER THROUGH THE GRASS? Yes, it was a _snake_.

Well, he was having no luck finding his shadow at the pond, so he walked back into the forest. There to greet him was his fast hopping friend, with long ears. WHO DO THE LISTENERS THINK IT WAS? It as _Mrs. Rabbit_. Gregory asked Mrs. Rabbit where his shadow could be. She said, "Follow me, Gregory." Off they went. "Wait," Gregory said, "I see a huge shadow with long legs, maybe it's mine!" They stopped. Gregory and Mrs. Rabbit started laughing. WHO WAS THIS FOREST FRIEND? Gregory sure felt silly to think that the big shadow of the _deer_ was his. Gregory took another step. In front of him was a smaller shadow. Yes, this could be his. He looked closely. Oops, the shadow had six legs and was really small. WHAT ANIMAL DO THE LISTENERS THINK GREGORY SAW NOW? Once again Gregory felt very silly. This was a shadow of an _ant_.

Gregory kept looking. All of a sudden the sun shone brightly. Gregory looked off to his left side. What he saw was a black shadow. It scared him so much that he didn't have much time to think or even to say thank you to Mrs. Rabbit. He ran directly towards his burrow and scampered into it as quickly as he could. There he felt very secure and warm. After he had caught his breath, he realized that he had been tricked once again, _this time by his very own shadow._

*by Liz and Dick Wilmes*

# MITTEN MATCH

(Use Pattern Pages 192-193)

## YOU'LL NEED

2 lb metal coffee can with a plastic lid
1 piece of white posterboard
Permanent red marker
1 piece of slightly patterned Contact® paper approximately 7"x22"
10" of magnetic tape.
Clear Contact® paper/laminating if available

## TO MAKE MITTEN MATCH

**Game Can**

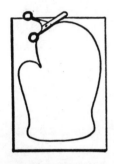

1. Cut a 2¼"x3" rectangle from the piece of posterboard. Trace a mitten shape on it. Cut out the mitten.

2. Keeping the backing sheet fastened to the Contact® paper, wrap it around the can to make sure that it fits. Trim any excess paper from the length, not the width, because it wraps over the top and inside of the can.

3. Lay your piece of Contact® paper, colored side up, flat on the table. Using the mitten pattern and the red marker, trace 10 mitten shapes on the paper. Draw a different, simple design on each mitten.

4. Carefully take the backing sheet off of the Contact® paper and wrap it paper around the coffee can. Wrap the excess paper over the top and inside of the can.

5. Using the excess Contact® paper, cut out a circle to fit on the top of the plastic lid. Using your mitten pattern, trace a mitten on the circle. Print "Mitten Match" on it. Attach the circle to the lid of the can.

**Game Pieces**

1. Using your mitten pattern, draw 10 mittens on the white posterboard and cut them out.

2. On each mitten draw a design which matches one of those on the game can.

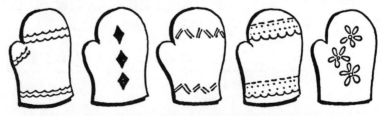

Mitten
Match

69

**Protect Your Game**

1. Laminate the Mittens or cover both sides of each one with clear Contact® paper.

2. Cut your magnetic tape into 10 equal pieces. Glue one magnetic piece to the back of each mitten.

3. Store the mittens inside the game can.

# TO PLAY <u>MITTEN MATCH</u>

1. Lay all of the mittens near the can.

2. Point to one mitten on the can and find its mate. Stick it on the can.

3. Continue until all of the mittens have been paired.

### *While Playing Talk About*
~ The designs on the player's mittens.
~ When the players wear mittens.
~ Playing in the snow.

## TO VARY YOUR GAME

♦ **COLOR MITTENS:** Make your game with a 3 lb coffee can. Use a larger mitten shape and make the mittens different colors so the players are pairing mittens by color instead of design.

♦♦ **LOOK AND MATCH:** To play the game, turn all of the mitten pieces over, so that they are face down. Turn one over and find its mate on the can. Turn the next one over and pair it. Continue until all of the mittens have been matched on the can.

♦♦♦ **LOOK CAREFULLY:** Make the designs on the mittens with more detail.

# FOOD TRAIN

(Use Pattern Pages 194-203)

## YOU'LL NEED

1 piece of colored posterboard
1 piece of black, yellow, orange, red, and blue construction paper
16, 1¼" colored dots
Lightweight cardboard/tagboard
Small magazine or drawn pictures of a variety of foods in 6 different categories:
    meats/fish, vegetables, fruits, sweets, dairy, and breads
X-Acto knife
2 metal rings
Clear Contact® paper/laminating if available

## TO MAKE FOOD TRAIN

**Game Board**

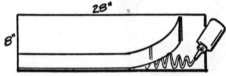

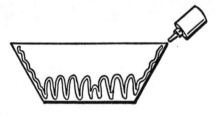

1. Cut 2, 8"x28" rectangles from your piece of posterboard.

2. To make the train tracks, cut the piece of lightweight cardboard into 2, 1½"x28" strips. Glue them along the bottoms of the 2 pieces of posterboard.

3. Using various colors of construction paper, trace a simple engine, caboose, and 6 train cars. Each one should be approximately 6" or 7" long. Cut them out.

4. Glue the engine on the left side of the first board and the caboose at the right end of the second board. Carefully brush glue along the 2 sides and bottom half of each train car and glue them equally spaced along the remaining track. The top half of the train cars should be left unglued on each board.

5. Add wheels by sticking 2 colored dots on the engine, caboose, and each of the train cars.

6. Glue one food picture on each train car to represent the 6 food categories.

7. Punch 2 holes at the end of the first board and 2 matching holes at the beginning of the second board.

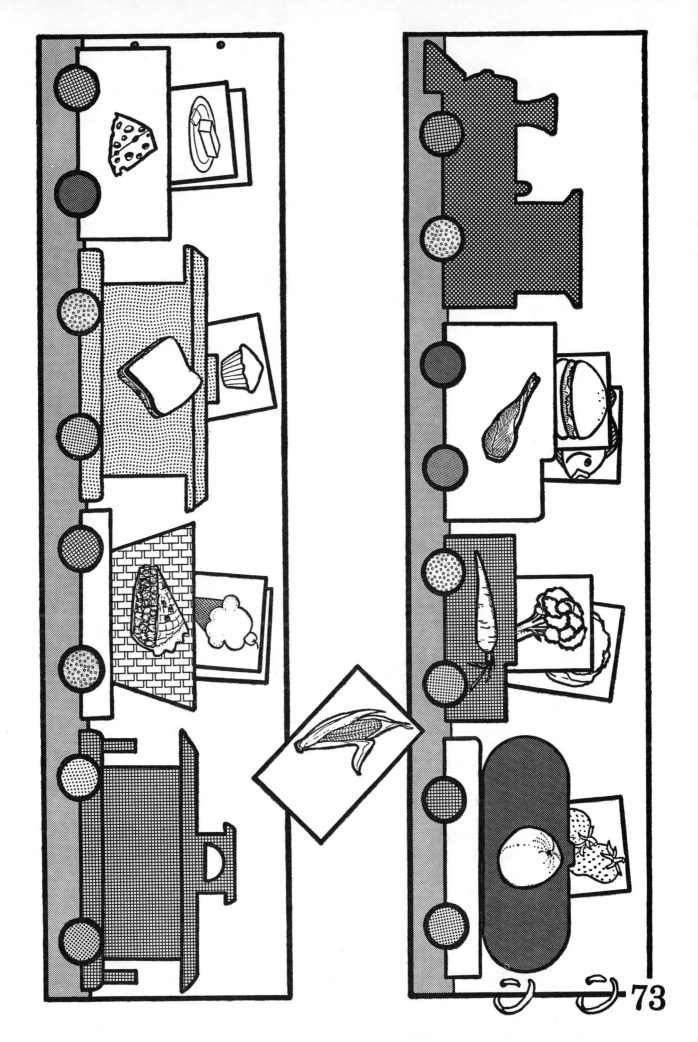

73

**Game Cards**

1. Cut the lightweight cardboard into 3"x6" cards.

2. Glue one food picture to the top half of each card.

**Protect Your Game**

1. Laminate the game or cover both sides of the Train and Food Cards with clear Contact® paper.

2. Carefully slit open the top of each train car to make a pocket.

3. Re-punch the 4 holes in the game boards. Attach them with the metal rings.

4. Store the game cards in several of the train cars or in a plastic bag which you can attach to one of the rings.

## TO PLAY <u>FOOD TRAIN</u>

1. Lay the train on the floor or table. Take out the food cards.

2. Look at the first card, decide what kind of food it is (meat/fish, vegetable, fruit, sweet, dairy, bread), and slip it into the appropriate car.

3. Continue until all of the food cards have been sorted.

*While Playing Talk About*
- ~ The players' favorite foods in each group.
- ~ Colors of the different foods.
- ~ What foods the players help to prepare.
- ~ Where different foods come from, such as apples from trees.

# TO VARY YOUR GAME

♦ **EASIER SORT:** When constructing the game, make only 2-4 train cars, each of them a little larger, along with a larger engine and caboose. Separate the food into 2-4 categories, maybe meat and grains or vegetables, fruits, and grains. Sort the cards into the appropriate train cars.

♦♦ **WILD CARDS:** When constructing the game, divide the food groups into 5 categories. Make the sixth group a "wild" one, that is, things which do not belong in any of the food groups. To play, put the food cards in the appropriate train cars, and the wild cards in the "wild car."

♦♦♦ **LONG FOOD TRAIN:** When constructing the game train, make an extra set of 4 train cars. Now the game cards can be sorted into 10 categories. You could add a drink, a condiment, a snack, and a fish car.

You might also print the name of each category on the train car.

# RAINDROP-SPLASH!

(Use Pattern Pages 204-206)

## YOU'LL NEED

1 piece of colored posterboard
1 piece of white posterboard
3 pieces of gray construction paper
Set of colored markers
Permanent black marker
1 piece of lightweight cardboard/tagboard
Clear Contact® paper/laminating if available

## TO MAKE RAINDROP-SPLASH!

**Game Board**

22"

14"

1. Cut a 14"x22" rectangle from your large piece of colored posterboard.

2. Trace 12 simple recognizable splashes on gray construction paper so that they all fit comfortable on the piece of posterboard. Cut each one out.

3. After making the game pieces (see below), glue the splashes to the posterboard.

4. After the glue has dried, outline each splash with black marker.

**Game Pieces**

1. Using the 12 figures that you made for splashes, trace and cut out another set from your white posterboard. (Glue the gray splashes to the board.)

2. Add details and color to each of your posterboard figures.

**Storage Pocket**

1. Cut a 4"x8" rectangle from your piece of lightweight cardboard/tagboard.

2. Curve the bottom corners to look like a pocket. Add detail.

3. Drizzle glue along the sides and bottom edge of the pocket and fasten it to the back of the game board.

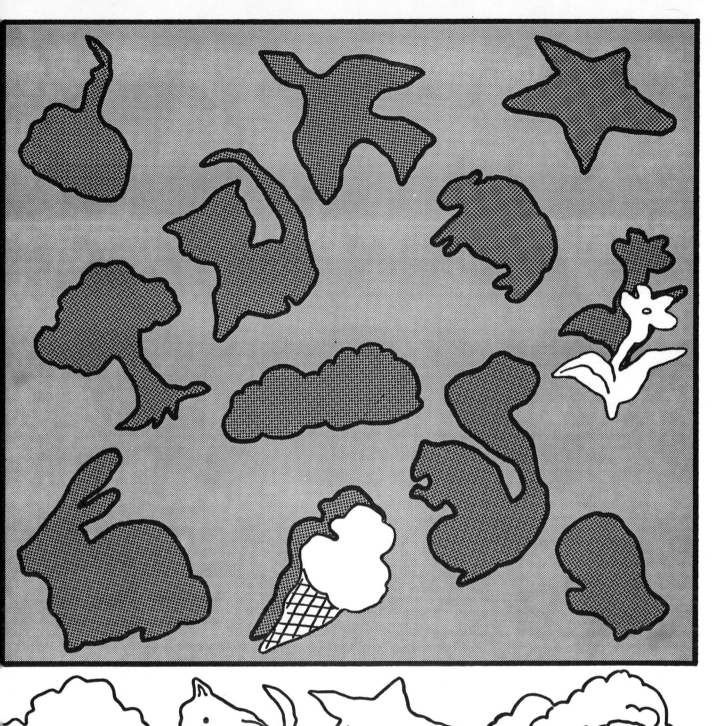

**Protect Your Game**
1. Laminate the game or cover both sides of the Game Board and the Pieces with clear Contact® paper.

2. Carefully slit open the top edge of your storage pocket.

3. Store the game pieces in the pocket.

# TO PLAY <u>RAINDROP-SPLASH!</u>

1. Lay the figures near the board.

2. Choose one figure. Look at all of the splashes and find the one that matches the figure. Lay it down.

3. Continue until all of the splashes have been matched with their figures.

### While Playing Talk About
~ What the splashes remind the players of.
~ Catching raindrops.
~ Splashing in puddles.
~ Clothes the players could wear to keep dry.

# TO VARY YOUR GAME

♦ **IDENTICAL MATCH:** When constructing the game, make the game pieces from gray posterboard to exactly match the splashes. Do not add any detail. To play simply match identical splashes.

♦♦ **LOOK CAREFULLY:** Make the game board slightly more difficult by not outlining each splash with a black marker.

♦♦♦ **MAKE YOUR OWN MATCHES:** Instead of making figures to correspond with the splashes, find pictures of the figures in magazines. Cut them out and back them with lightweight cardboard. Match the different pictures with the splashes.

# GIVE GERI GIRAFFE HER SPOTS

(Use Pattern Page 207)

## YOU'LL NEED

1 piece of colored posterboard
1, 12"x26" piece of yellow shelf paper or butcher paper
1 piece of brown posterboard
1 small piece of white posterboard
Brown and black markers
1 metal brad
Clear Contact® paper/laminating if available

## TO MAKE <u>GERI GIRAFFE</u>

**Game Board**

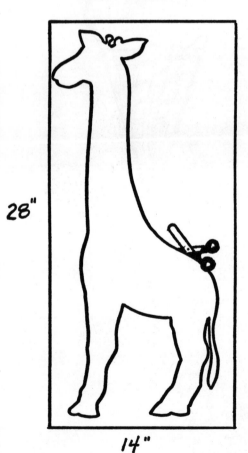

28"

14"

1. Cut a 14"x28" rectangle from your piece of colored posterboard.

2. Using the black marker, draw a simple giraffe shape on the yellow paper. Cut her out. Glue her to the colored posterboard.

3. From your piece of brown posterboard trace and cut out:

    1, 2½"x 3½" rectangle
    1, 2¼"x3" rectangle
    1, 1"x3" rectangle
    1, 2½" square
    1, 1½" square
    1, 1" square
    1, 2" circle
    1, 1½" circle
    1, 1" circle
    1, 2¾"x2¾"x2¾" triangle
    1, 2"x2"x2" triangle
    1, 1½"x1½"x1½" triangle

4. Lay the brown shapes on the yellow giraffe. Using your brown marker, trace around each shape.

83

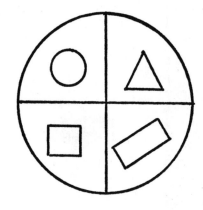

5. To make the shape wheel draw a 5" circle to the right of Geri's neck. Divide the circle into quarters. Trace a circle, a square, a triangle, and a rectangle in the 4 sections.

6. To make the spinner cut a 1"x3" rectangle from the piece of white posterboard. Trace a 3"x3"x1" triangle on it. Cut it out.

7. Using the black marker, add details to your giraffe.

**Game Pieces**

1. The 12 brown shapes which you used for patterns to make Geri's spots are your game pieces.

**Storage Pocket**

1. Cut a 4"x6" rectangle from the lightweight cardboard. Round corners to look like a pocket. Add details.

2. Drizzle glue along the 2 sides and bottom edge of the pocket and fasten it to the back of the folder.

**Protect Your Game**

1. Laminate the game or cover both sides of the Game Board, Shapes, and Spinner with clear Contact® paper.

2. Loosely attach the spinner to the middle of the shape wheel with a brad.

3. Carefully slit open the top edge of the pocket.

4. Store Geri's spots in it.

## TO PLAY GERI GIRAFFE

1. Lay Geri's spots near her.

2. Have the first player flick the spinner. When it stops, name the shape. Find one of those shapes and match it to one of Geri's spots. The second player flicks the spinner and adds another spot to Geri. Continue until Geri has all of her spots.

***While Playing Talk About***
- Freckles that the players might have.
- Do the players freckles look like Geri's spots?
- Trips to the zoo.
- Tall people whom the players know.

# TO VARY YOUR GAME

♦ **EASY MATCH:** When making your game board, color Geri's spots so that they are solid brown rather than just an outline.

♦ **GIVE GERI HER SPOTS:** When making your game board do not give Geri any spots. To play, each player flicks the spinner and lays the designated shape wherever he wants on Geri.

♦♦♦ **CRAZY SPOTS:** When making the game board, give Geri more complicated spots. Remember to make your shape wheel correspond with the new shapes.

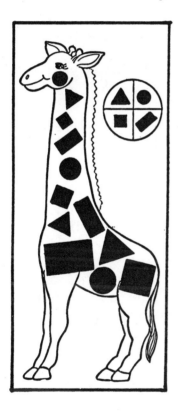 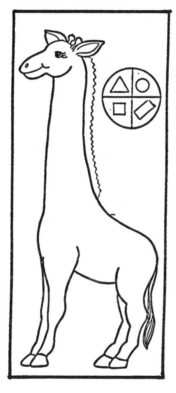 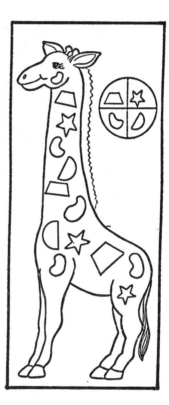

# MINI DINO JUMP

### (Use Pattern Pages 208-211)

## YOU'LL NEED

4 pieces of different colored posterboard
52, ¾" round dots in 5-6 different colors
1 small piece of white posterboard
4 metal brads
Permanent black marker
Clear Contact® paper/laminating if available

## TO MAKE <u>MINI DINO JUMP</u>

**Game Boards**

1. Cut an 11"x14" rectangle from each of your pieces of colored posterboard.

2. Enlarge the pattern/s and then trace a simple dinosaur on each rectangle. They can be the same or different dinosaurs. Cut each one out.

3. Add a trail of colored dots along each dinosaur's back. Remember to mix up the colors. If you want, draw and color several dino prints along the way to break up the dotted path.

4. To make the number wheel, draw a 3½" circle in the middle of each dinosaur. Divide each one into quarters. Write numeral "1" in the first section, "2" in the second, and so on.

5. To make the spinner, cut a 1½"x3½" rectangle out of the white posterboard. Draw a dinosaur bone on it. Cut it out. Draw an arrow down the middle.

6. Add details to your dinosaurs.

**Protect Your Game**

1. Laminate the game or cover both sides of each Dinosaur and the Spinners with clear Contact® paper.

2. Attach the spinners to the middle of the number wheels with brads.

# TO PLAY MINI DINO JUMP

1. Give each player a mover. Small dinosaur erasers work well.

2. Have the first player flick the spinner on his dinosaur. When the spinner stops, name the number. The player walks his mover along the dinosaur's back the appropriate amount of spaces. Each player flicks the spinner and moves along his dinosaur's back in the same manner. If a player stops on a dino print, he walks ahead one space.

3. Continue until everyone has walked to the end of his dinosaur's tail.

*While Playing Talk About*
- ~ Dinosaurs.
- ~ How to count spaces.
- ~ How dinosaurs might have moved and what sounds they could have made.

# TO VARY YOUR GAME

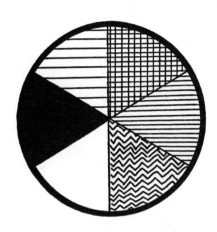

♦ **COLOR WALK:** Using the colors you chose for the dots, divide your wheel by colors instead of numbers.

♦♦ **COME BACK MR. DINO:** After a player has moved to the end of the dinosaur's tail, have the player turn around and move back up the dinosaur to his head.

♦♦♦ **BACKWARDS AND FORWARDS:** When constructing the trail along the dinosaurs' backs, add more dots and draw in several more dino prints. On each print, write "1" or "2." When playing, if a player lands on a dino print with "1" written on it, he moves back 1 space. If he lands on "2" he moves back 2 spaces.

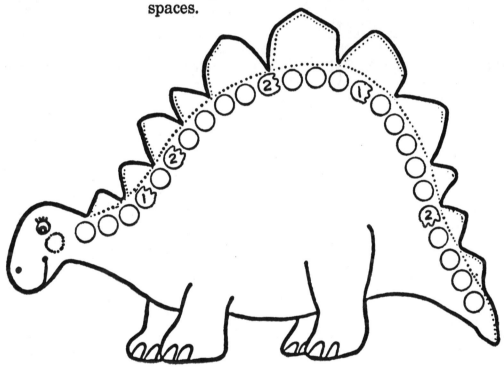

# COPY CAT

### (Use Pattern Pages 212-213)

## YOU'LL NEED

1 piece of colored posterboard
1 piece of white posterboard
1 metal ring
Permanent black marker
Washable marker
Ruler
Paper punch
Clear Contact® paper/laminating if available

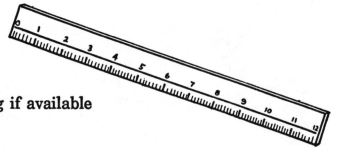

## TO MAKE <u>COPY CAT</u>

**Front-Back Covers**

1. Cut 2, 7"x9" rectangles from your piece of colored posterboard. One will be the front cover and the other one will be the back cover.

2. On one rectangle trace a simple outline of a cat's face. Cut it out. Add the cat's facial features.

3. On the other rectangle, use your cat pattern to trace another cat. Cut it out. Add a tail.

**Book Pages**

1. Cut 7, 7"x9" rectangles from your piece of white construction paper.

2. Using one of your cat patterns, trace and cut out 7 cat pages.

3. With your black marker and a ruler, vertically divide each cat page in half.

4. On the left half of each page, draw the line or pattern you want the player to copy.

5. Punch a hole near the ear on the left side of each cat. Clip the pages together with the medal ring binder.

**Protect Your Book**

1. Laminate the book or cover both sides of the Front and Back Covers and all of the Book Pages with clear Contact® paper.

2. Re-punch the holes.

3. Arrange the pages in order and add the front and back cover.

4. Clip the book together with the metal ring.

## TO PLAY <u>COPY CAT</u>

1. Have a washable marker and small clean cloth.

2. Open the book to the first page and look at the marking on the left side.

3. With your marker, copy the marking in the empty space.

4. Continue until you have copied each marking in Copy Cat's book.

5. With the cloth, wipe off your markings so that Copy Cat is ready for the next player.

### While Playing Talk About
~ The line or shape Copy Cat is asking you to make.
~ Pet cats that the players might have.

# TO VARY YOUR GAME

♦ **COLOR AND ERASE:** Change the purpose of the book from copying lines and shapes to copying colors. To make the book cut 8 or more cat pages. On the left side of each page, make a large scribble with a different color marker. Protect the pages.

Give the player a set of colored washable markers that match the colors in the book and let him copy the colors. When finished, he should wipe off his colored scribbles, so that the book is ready for the next player.

♦ **TRACING FUN:** Instead of copying the marks on each page of your Copy Cat Book, trace over the ones already drawn in the book with your pointer finger or a washable marker. Remember to wipe the book clean if you used a marker.

♦♦ **DRAW YOUR OWN MARKS:** When constructing the book do not make any markings on the left side of each page. Simply divide each one in half.

To Play: You'll need 2 players. Give each player a set of washable markers and a cloth. Have one player make any type of marking he wants on the left side. Let the other player copy it. Encourage the players to continue through the book. Wipe the book clean. Switch places and play again.

♦♦♦ **WRITING LETTERS AND MORE:** When constructing the book, instead of drawing lines and shapes on each page, write letters, numerals, or abstract markings. Increase and decrease the number of pages as is appropriate for your children.

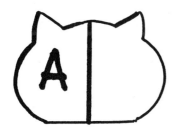  

# COLOR BINGO

(Use Pattern Page 214)

## YOU'LL NEED

1 piece of white duplicating paper
Fine-tipped permanent black marker
9 different colored markers
Ruler
1 piece of lightweight cardboard/tagboard
Clear Contact® paper/laminating if available
1 large resealable plastic bag

## TO MAKE <u>COLOR BINGO</u>

**Bingo Cards**

1. Using your permanent black marker, draw a 8¼"x8¼" square on the duplicating paper.

2. Divide the large square into 9 equal squares, each 2¾"x2¾".

3. Trace a simple crayon shape in the 3 squares in the first column, a balloon shape in the squares in the middle column, and paint brushes in the third column.

4. Decide how many bingo cards you want. Duplicate the basic pattern that many times. Trim the grids so that they are all 8¼" square. Save the original pattern.

5. Color the crayons, balloons, and paint brushes on each of the grids with the colored markers. Do not duplicate the sequence of colors in any column.

6. Cut the lightweight cardboard into as many 9"x9" squares as you have bingo grids. Glue one cardboard square to the back of each bingo grid.

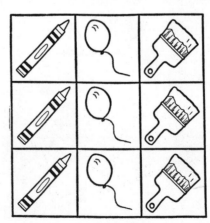

**Game Pieces**

1. Duplicate the original bingo pattern 3 more times.

2. Using your colored markers, color one crayon, balloon, and paint brush with each of the nine colors.

3. Cut the grids into individual squares.

4. Cut 27, 3"x3" squares from the lightweight cardboard. Glue one square to the back of each game piece.

**Protect Your Game**

1. Laminate the game or cover both sides of the Bingo Cards and Game Pieces with clear Contact® paper.

2. Store the game in the resealable bag.

## TO PLAY <u>COLOR BINGO</u>

1. Give each player a bingo card and some bingo chips. (You could make your own chips by gluing 2" colored dots on lightweight cardboard.)

2. Turn all of the game pieces over. Pick up one card and call out what it is, such as "red balloon".

3. All players who have a "red balloon" on their cards should cover it up with a chip.

4. Continue until the players have covered all of their colored pictures.

*While Playing Talk About*
   ~ Different colors.
   ~ Times that the players have flown balloons.
   ~ Adults they know who play bingo.
   ~ What colors the players like to color with.

# TO VARY YOUR GAME

♦ **STRIP MATCH:** Construct a simple matching game. To make, cut 3, 3"x24" strips of white posterboard. Divide each strip into 8, 3 inch squares. In each square on the first strip draw a balloon. Color them 8 different colors. Make 8 matching balloon pieces. Make the second strip and pieces with crayons, and the third one with paint brushes.

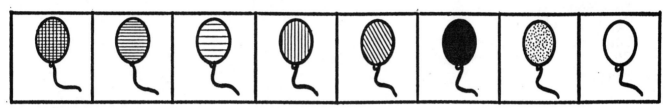

♦♦♦ **LOOK CAREFULLY:** When playing the game, give each player a bingo card. Lay all of the game pieces face down on the table or floor. Let the first player turn a piece over, look at the picture, and see if he has a matching one on his card. If he does, he lays it on his bingo card; if not, he puts it back in the group face down. Continue until all of the pieces have been matched.

♦♦♦ **BINGO:** Play the game more like conventional bingo. Instead of playing until each player has covered his card, play until a player has covered 3 crayons, brushes, and/or balloons in a row, column, or diagonal.

# LACING NUMBERS

(Use Pattern Pages 215-219)

## YOU'LL NEED

1 piece posterboard
10 pieces of construction paper
Yarn/shoe laces
Paper punch
Large resealable plastic bag
Clear Contact$^R$ paper/laminating if available
Metal ring

## TO MAKE <u>LACING NUMBERS</u>

**Number Cards**

1. Cut 10, 5"x7" pieces of posterboard.

2. Trace a large number shape (0-9) on each piece. Cut out each number.

3. Cut slightly smaller construction paper number shapes. Glue the smaller shape on top of the larger shape.

4. Punch holes through the middle of each number.

98

**Protect Your Game**

1. Laminate the Numbers or cover both sides of each one with clear Contact[R] paper.

2. Cut each number again and re-punch the holes.

3. Cut 10 appropriate lengths of yarn. Make a point at one end of each piece by taping it or dipping it in clear fingernail polish. Tie the other end to the first hole at the top of each number card. (Use shoe laces if it would be easier for your children.)

4. Store the LACING NUMBERS in the resealable bag. Attach a metal ring and hang it on a low hook in your room.

# TO PLAY <u>LACING NUMBERS</u>

1. Put some or all of the lacing numbers on a large tray. Set the tray on the table or floor.

2. Let the children choose numbers and lace and unlace them as they choose.

*While Playing Talk About*
~ The names of the numbers which the players are lacing.
~ Numbers the players see around the room.
~ How old the players are. Their brothers and sisters.

# TO VARY THE GAME

♦ **FOLLOW THE NUMBER:** Make number shapes without holes. Lay them on the table/floor with a container of small blocks, checkers, or poker chips. Players can line up the markers on the number shapes.

♦ **TEXTURED NUMBERS:** Make a series of sandpaper or heavy wallpaper numbers and hang them on a wall at the children's eye level. Encourage the children to trace the numbers with their fingers.

♦♦ **COVER THE DOTS:** Make number shapes without holes. Using a black marker, draw the appropriate number of dots on each number. Lay them on the table/floor with a container of bingo chips. Let the players match the chips to the dots on each number.

♦♦♦ **NUMBER STENCILS:** Make number shapes without holes. Put the numbers on a table with paper, markers, and colored pencils. Let the children use them for giant stencils.

# I SPY

(Use Pattern Pages 220-224)

## YOU'LL NEED

3 colored file folders
3 pieces of white paper
9 small pictures related to a farm
9 small pictures related to a beach
9 small pictures related to a beach
12-18 miscellaneous pictures
Set of markers or crayons
Permanent black marker
1 piece of lightweight cardboard/tagboard
Clear Contact® paper/laminating if available

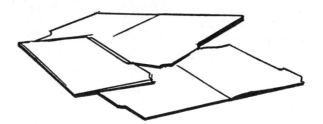

## TO MAKE I SPY

**Game Board**

1. On one piece of white paper draw an 8¼"x8¼" square. Make a grid by dividing the square into 9 equal, 2¾"x2¾" squares.

2. Duplicate, color, and glue the city, farm, beach, and miscellaneous pictures (wild cards) to the squares.

3. Print "farm" in the space above the grid.

4. Make identical folders for the "city" and "beach".

**Game Cards**

1. Cut 45, 2½"x2½" squares from the piece of lightweight cardboard.

2. Glue the city, farm, beach, and miscellaneous pictures (wild cards) to the squares.

102

farm

I SPY "FARM"

103

| Storage Pockets | 1. Cut 3, 4"x6" rectangles from the piece of lightweight cardboard. Round the bottom corners. |
| | 2. On the farm pocket trace a farm animal, the beach pocket a beach ball, and the city pocket a traffic light. |
| | 3. Drizzle glue along the sides and bottom edge of each pocket and fasten each to the middle of the left side of the appropriate file folder. |

**Front Covers**

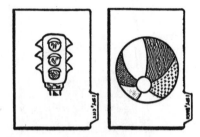

1. Trace a picture of a simple farm animal, beach ball, and traffic light on the appropriate front covers.

2. Print the name of the games on the appropriate folder tabs.

**Protect Your Game**

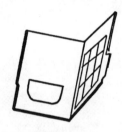

1. Laminate the games or cover both sides of the 3 File Folders and all of the Game Cards with clear Contact® paper.

2. Carefully slit open the top edges of your pockets.

3. Store the appropriate cards plus 4-6 wild cards in each of your storage pockets.

# TO PLAY I SPY

1. Choose the farm, city or beach file folder.

2. Open it and take out all of the game cards.

3. Look at the first card. Does it remind you of a farm (city, beach)? If so put the card on one of the squares in the grid. If not, put it back in the storage pocket.

4. Continue until you have found all of the farm pictures (city, beach) and laid them on the grid.

***While Playing Talk About***
 ~ Trips the players have taken to the farm, city, or beach.
 ~ What is being pictured on each card.
 ~ What jobs people do on a farm, in a city, or at a beach.
 ~ Safety rules for the farm, city, and beach.

104

# TO VARY YOUR GAME

♦ **NAME IT:** When constructing the game make only the 9 game cards which are appropriate to each scene. To play simply look at each game card, identify it, and lay it on the grid.

♦♦♦ **SORT THE CARDS:** When constructing the game, glue a blank grid on the left and right hand side of the file folder. Above one grid print "farm" and above the other one print "beach." Put the storage pocket on the backside. Trace a beach ball/barn on the front side. Use the game cards from the farm and beach, no wild cards.

To play, mix up the cards. Look at the first one. Does it remind you of the farm or beach? Lay it on the appropriate grid. Continue until all of the cards have been sorted.

# IN THE BARN

(Use Pattern Pages 225-226)

## YOU'LL NEED

1 piece of red posterboard
2 pieces of white duplicating paper
2 pieces of yellow construction paper
2 pieces of blue construction paper
9-12 pictures of different farm animals which you can easily duplicate
1 small piece of lightweight cardboard/tagboard
Permanent black marker
Clear Contact® paper/laminating if available

## TO MAKE IN THE BARN

**Game Board**

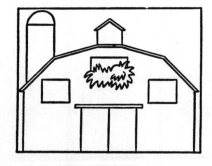

1. Cut your piece of red posterboard into a 19"x22" rectangle.

2. Using your black marker, draw a large barn. On each side of the barn draw 2 large windows, approximately 3"x4". You might cut out a yellow hay stack and glue it in a loft window.

**Game Cards**

1. Duplicate the farm animal cards twice. Color them.

2. Cut them out.

106

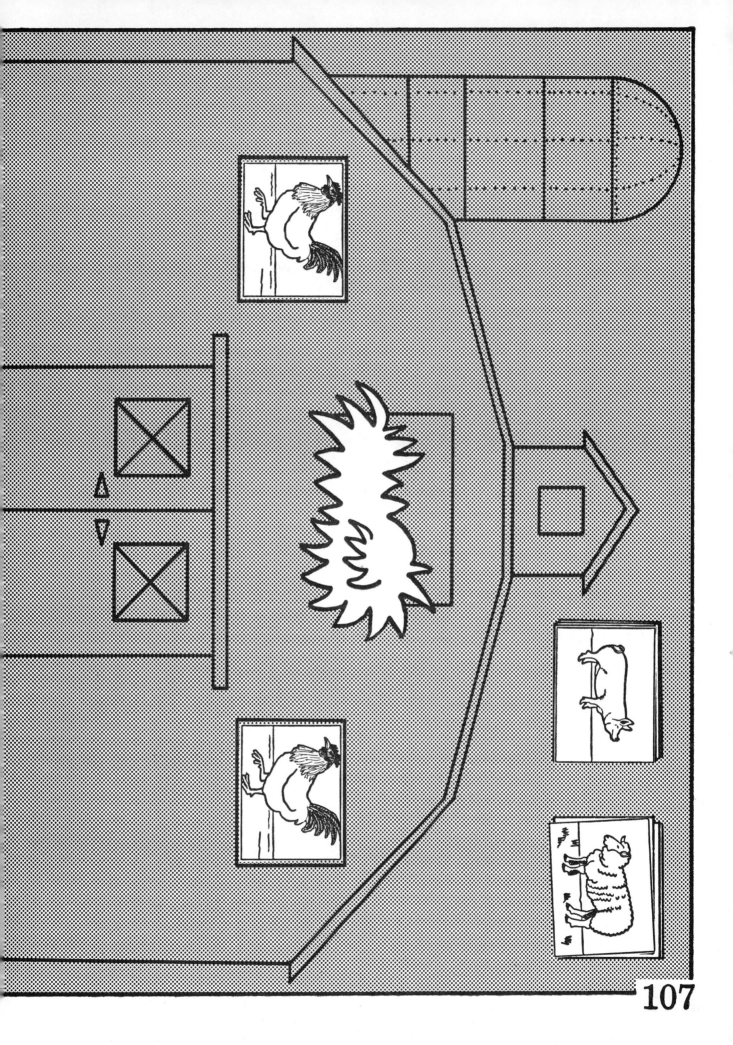

3. Cut 6, 2¾"x3¾" rectangles from each piece of colored construction paper.

4. Glue one set of farm animal pictures to the yellow construction paper cards and the other set to the blue cards.

**Storage Pockets**

1. Cut 2, 4"x6" rectangles from the piece of lightweight cardboard.

2. Round the bottom corners to look like pockets. Add detail.

3. Drizzle glue along the sides and bottom edges of the pockets and fasten them to the back of the game board.

**Protect Your Game**

1. Laminate the game or cover both sides of the Game Board and Animal Cards with clear Contact® paper.

2. Carefully slit open the top edges of the 2 storage pockets.

3. Store one set of animal cards in each pocket.

# TO PLAY <u>IN THE BARN</u>

1. Give each player one set of animal cards.

2. The first player lays one of his cards on a barn window.

3. The second player looks through all of his cards until he finds the one that matches and then lays it on the other barn window.

4. The first player lays another animal card down and the second player finds the mate from his stack and lays it down.

5. Continue until all of the animal cards are matched.

*While Playing Talk About*
   ~ The names of the animals.
   ~ Sounds that the animals make.
   ~ Trips the children have taken to a farm.
   ~ Farm animals the children might have seen at the zoo.

# TO VARY YOUR GAME

♦ **EASIER MATCH:** Construct the game with fewer animal cards in each set.

♦♦ **NAME THAT ANIMAL:** Construct the game with only one set of animal pictures. Have the player look at the first card, name it, and lay it down on a barn window.

♦♦♦ **ADULTS WITH THEIR BABIES:** When constructing the game, make one set of adult farm animals and a set of matching baby farm animals, such as a horse and a foal, a pig and a piglet, a cow and a calf, and so on.

SUMMER

# FAVORITE FLAVORS

(Use Pattern Page 227)

## YOU'LL NEED

1 colored file folder
1 piece each of light brown/tan, purple, orange, brown, black, yellow, red, green, and white construction paper
Set of colored markers to match your construction paper (except tan)
1 piece of lightweight cardboard/tagboard
2 metal brads
Clear Contact® paper/laminating if available

## TO MAKE <u>FAVORITE FLAVORS</u>

**Game Board**

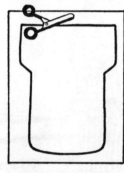

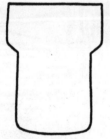

1. Cut 2, 4"x5" rectangles from the piece of tan construction paper. Trace an ice cream cone shape on each one and cut it out.

2. Open the file folder and turn it the long way. Glue the 2 cones near the bottom edge of the folder.

3. Make a Color Wheel. (See CLIP IT, page 30.)

**Game Pieces**

1. Duplicate the largest size scoop.

2. Using the scoop for a pattern make 2 sets of different colored construction paper scoops.

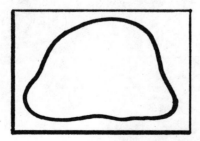
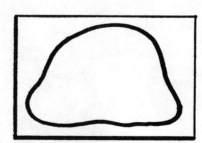

Favorite Flavors

**Storage Pocket**

1. Cut a 4"x8" rectangle from the piece of lightweight cardboard. Round the bottom corners. Add details.

2. Drizzle glue along the sides and bottom edge of the pocket and fasten it to the middle of the backside of the folder.

**Front Cover**

1. Using your construction paper make a double or triple dip ice cream cone. Glue it to the center of the folder.

2. Write the name of the game on the folder tab.

**Protect Your Game**

1. Laminate the game or cover both sides of the File Folder and all of the Scoops with clear Contact paper.

2. Carefully slit open the top edge of your storage pocket.

3. Store the scoops in your storage pocket.

## TO PLAY <u>FAVORITE FLAVORS</u>

1. Give each player a set of ice cream scoops.

2. The first player flicks his spinner. When it stops, he looks at the color, and decides if he wants that flavor on his cone. If he does, he adds the scoop to his cone; if he doesn't, he puts the scoop off to the side. The second player flicks his spinner and begins to build his ice cream cone in the same way.

3. At anytime during the game, either player can add the vanilla scoop to his cone.

4. Continue until both players have built cones with their favorite flavors.

*While Playing Talk About*
   ~ Times the players have eaten real ice cream cones.
   ~ The players favorite flavors.
   ~ Where the players eat ice cream.

# TO VARY YOUR GAME

♦ **CHOOSE FLAVORS:** When constructing your game, do not use the spinner. Let each player simply choose a flavor he wants and then put it on his cone. Talk about the colors and flavors as each player adds his scoops.

♦♦ **HIGHER AND HIGHER CONES:** To play "Higher and Higher" put all of the scoops in the middle. When a player flicks a certain color he takes the scoop from a common pile. He may end up with 1 or 2 scoops of some flavors and none of others.

♦♦♦ **TRIPLE DIP PLEASE:** Instead of letting each player build as tall a cone as he would like, limit the players to 3 scoops. Thus when a player flicks the spinner, he'll have to decide if that flavor is one of his 3 favorites. If so he adds it to his cone; if not he puts it off to the side.

♦♦♦ **LARGE TO SMALL SCOOPS:** Trace and cut out different size scoops. Let the children build ice cream cones going from largest to smallest scoops or smallest to largest.

# HAPPY BIRTHDAY

(Use Pattern Pages 228-232)

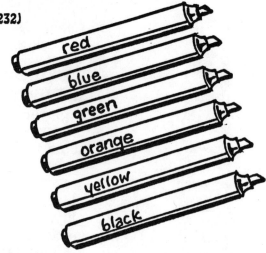

## YOU'LL NEED

1 colored file folder
3 pieces of light colored construction paper
16 plain white index cards
Set of colored markers
1 piece of lightweight cardboard/tagboard
Clear Contact® paper/laminating if available

## TO MAKE HAPPY BIRTHDAY

**Game Board**

1. On one piece of construction paper, trace a birthday cake pattern to fit on one side of the file folder. Cut it out.

2. Using the pattern, trace 2 more cakes on the other pieces of construction paper and cut them out.

3. On one birthday cake print, "Happy Birthday". Draw several identical stars along the bottom for trim.
    On a second cake print, "Happy Birthday". Draw several stars along the bottom, all of which are different.
    Decorate the third cake however you'd like.
    Color the cakes, remembering to color the identical stars on the first cake the same color.

4. Open the file folder. Carefully brush glue along the sides and bottom half of the first two cakes. Glue the cake with identical stars to the left side of the folder, and the one with different stars to the right side. Save the third one.

**Game Cards**

1. Divide the index cards into 2 piles of 8 each. On the first set of 8 cards duplicate, color, and glue 2 identical birthday hats, cakes, horns, presents, candles, ice cream cones, balloons, and cards.

2. On the second set of 8 cards, duplicate, color, and glue color 2 different birthday hats, cakes, horns, presents, candles, ice cream cones, balloons, and cards.

116

**Storage Pocket**

1. Cut a 4"x8" rectangle from your piece of lightweight cardboard. Round the bottom corners.

2. Drizzle glue along the sides and bottom edge of the pocket and fasten it to the back of the folder.

**Front Cover**

1. Glue the third birthday cake to the front cover. Add candles to it.

2. Print the name of the game on the folder tab.

**Protect Your Game**

1. Laminate the game or cover both sides of the File Folder and the Game Cards with clear Contact® paper.

2. Carefully slit the top edge of your storage pocket and the 2 inside birthday cakes.

3. Store the game cards in your storage pocket.

# TO PLAY <u>HAPPY BIRTHDAY</u>

1. Take the game cards out of the storage pocket. Open the folder and lay the cards near it.

2. Pick up the first card and decide if the two pictures on the card are the same or different. If they are the same, slip the card into the cake with the matching stars on it; if not, slip it into the cake with the different stars.

3. Continue until you've sorted all of the birthday cards into the "same" and "different" pockets.

*While Playing Talk About*
~ Birthday parties.
~ Singing the "Happy Birthday" song.
~ Blowing out candles.
~ How old each player is.

118

# TO VARY YOUR GAME

♦ **SORT THE CARDS:** Change the object of the game. Make cards which have pictures of things related to birthday parties and things which are not related to birthdays such as a comb, socks, banana, lamp, and so on.

To play, sort the cards by putting those pictures related to birthdays in the cake with the same stars and those pictures which the player does not think are related to birthdays in the cake with different stars.

♦♦ **PLAN A PARTY:** Change the object of the game to planning a birthday party. Make individual cards of different cakes, hats, candles, gifts, horns, balloons, etc.

To play look at the first card, for example a cake. Decide if you would like that cake for your birthday party. If so slip it into the cake with identical stars; if not, slip it into the cake with different stars. Continue with the other birthday pictures until they are all sorted. Then pull out all of the ones that you want at your party. Look at them. Make any changes you wish.

♦♦♦ **LOOK CAREFULLY:** When constructing the "same" and "different" cards use only one birthday symbol such as gifts or hats. Change only one detail to make the "different" cards.

**119**

# 1,2,3 LADYBUG

**(Use Pattern Page 233)**

## YOU'LL NEED

1 piece of red posterboard
1 piece of green posterboard
3 pieces of red construction paper
1 piece of lightweight cardboard/tagboard
Permanent black marker
Ruler
Clear Contact® paper/laminating if available

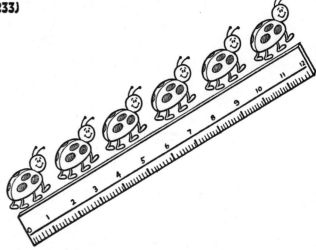

## TO MAKE <u>1,2,3 LADYBUG</u>

**Game Board**

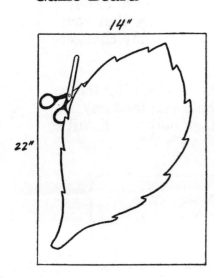

1. Cut a 14"x22" rectangle from your piece of green posterboard.

2. Draw a large, simple leaf shape on the rectangle and cut it out.

3. Duplicate and cut out the 4" ladybug pattern.

4. Using the ladybug pattern draw 10 circles on the red construction paper. Cut them out.

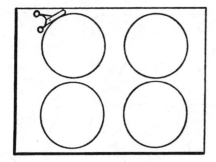 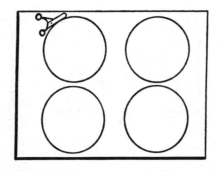 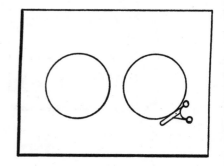

5. On the first red circle draw one, 1" dot (size of a quarter). Add facial features. On the second circle make two, 1" dots and so on. When you are making ladybugs with more than 5 dots reduce the size of her spots just a little.

6. Glue the ladybugs to the large leaf in random order.

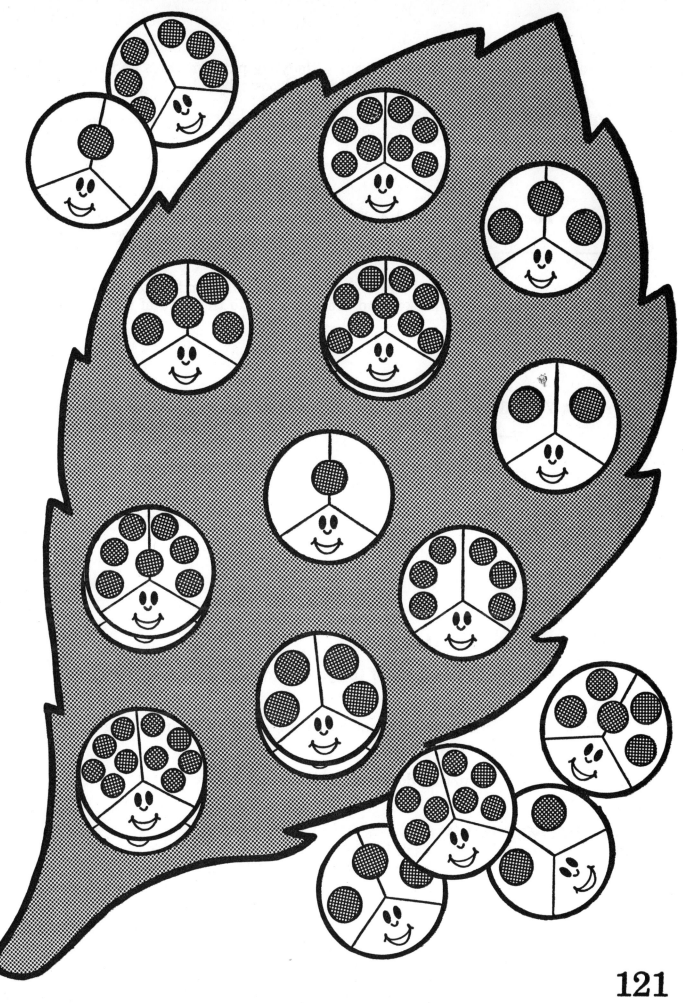

**Game Pieces**

1. Using your 4" ladybug pattern, trace and cut out 10 circles from your red posterboard.

2. Draw a matching ladybug from the game board on each circle.

**Storage Pocket**

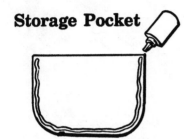

1. Cut a 6"x9" rectangle from the piece of lightweight cardboard/tagboard. Round the bottom corners. Add details.

2. Drizzle glue along the sides and bottom edge of the pocket and then fasten it to the back of the leaf.

**Protect Your Game**

1. Laminate the game or cover both sides of the Leaf and all of the Ladybugs with clear Contact® paper.

2. Carefuly slit open the top edge of your storage pocket.

3. Store the ladybugs in the storage pocket.

## TO PLAY 1,2,3 LADYBUG

1. Take the ladybugs out of the pocket and lay them near the game board.

2. Pick up one ladybug, count her spots, and find the matching ladybug on the leaf. Lay it down.

3. Continue counting dots and matching ladybugs until each one has a twin.

***While Playing Talk About***
~ How many spots each ladybug has.
~ Other creatures the children might see while playing outside.

# TO VARY YOUR GAME

♦ **SHAPE BUGS:** When making the ladybugs on the game board and each matching ladybug piece, draw a different shape on each one. Then have the players match the shapes which are alike.

♦ **EASY MATCH:** When constructing the game, make 5, 5" or 6" ladybugs instead of 10.

♦♦ **READING NUMBERS:** When making your game board and matching ladybugs write the numeral along with the spots on each one.

♦♦♦ **FEELING FACES:** When making your game board and matching ladybugs, draw all of them with the same amount of spots, but different facial features.

# FEELINGS CONCENTRATION

(Use Pattern Pages 234-238)

## YOU'LL NEED

2 each of drawn or magazine pictures showing 10 different feeling faces
Light weight cardboard or tagboard
Clear Contact$^R$ paper/laminating if available
Large resealable plastic bag
Metal ring

## TO MAKE FEELINGS CONCENTRATION

**Game Cards**

1. Cut 20, 4"x6" pieces of cardboard.

2. Cut out the feeling pictures. Glue one picture to each piece of cardboard.

**Protect Your Game**

1. Laminate the Feeling Cards or cover both sides of each card with clear Contact[R] paper.

2. Store the cards in a resealable bag. Attach a metal ring to the bag and hang it on a low hook in your room.

# TO PLAY <u>FEELINGS CONCENTRATION</u>

1. Take all of the cards out of the bag and lay them face up on the table/floor.

2. Mix up all of the cards. Name all of the feelings.

3. Have the children turn them all face down. Mix them around.

4. The first player turns two cards over. If they are a match, the player keeps them and plays again; if they are not a match, the player turns the cards back over and the next player turns two cards over.

5. Continue playing until all of the feeling faces have been paired.

***While Playing Talk About***
~ The names of the different feelings.
~ When the players may have felt like the people in the pictures.
~ Other people the players have seen who have felt like the people in the pictures.

# TO VARY THE GAME

♦ **FIND THAT FEELING:** Put all of the feeling cards face up on the table/floor. Say to the players, *"I'm looking for the 'sad boy' card."* When they see it they should point to it. Take it off of the table/floor. Continue until all of the cards have been identified.

♦♦ **MATCH THE FEELING FACES:** Make a matching game with the cards. Glue one feeling face from each pair of cards to a piece of posterboard. Laminate the gameboard or cover it with clear Contact[R] paper. Put the duplicate cards in a margarine tub.
    To play have a player pull one card out of the tub, look at it, find the mate on the board, and place the card on top of it. Continue until all of the feeling faces have been matched.

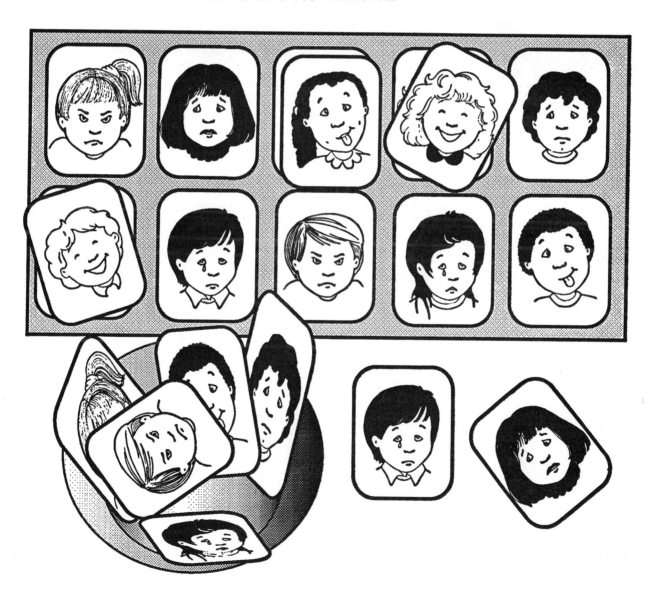

# WHISKERS SAYS

### (Use Pattern Pages 239-240)

## YOU'LL NEED

1 piece of white posterboard
5 large unlined pink index cards
Permanent black marker
X-acto knife
Clear Contact® paper/laminating if available

## TO MAKE <u>WHISKERS SAYS</u>

**Game Board**

1. Cut a 13"x18" rectangle from your piece of white posterboard.

2. Draw a very simple rabbit face on it and then cut it out.

3. Using a pink index card, draw and cut out pink trim for the ears. Glue them on.

4. Add facial features to your rabbit.

5. Carefully cut 4 one inch slits in each of the rabbit's cheeks for his whiskers. (Remember safety.)

**Game Pieces**

1. Cut 8, 6"x6"x1½" triangles from the pink index cards for the rabbit's whiskers.

2. Duplicate the figures doing the actions. Glue them to the rabbit's whiskers. Color them if you'd like.

**Protect Your Game**

1. Laminate the game or cover both sides of the Rabbit and each of its Whiskers with clear Contact® paper.

2. Re-cut each slit in the rabbit's cheeks.

3. Slip a whisker into each slit.

# TO PLAY WHISKERS SAYS

1. Hang Whiskers low on a wall near a full length mirror.

2. Pull out one of his whiskers. "Read" what Whiskers is telling you to do. Lay the whisker down.

3. Do the action several times.

4. Pull out another whisker, "read" it, and do that exercise.

5. Continue until you have pulled out all of the whiskers and done the actions.

6. Slip all of the whiskers back into the face so that the game is ready for the next player.

***While Playing Talk About***
- ~ What body parts you are using to do each action.
- ~ Doing actions quickly and slowly.
- ~ How the players know what action to do.

# TO VARY THE GAME

♦ **EXERCISE:** Instead of drawing a figure doing an action on each whisker, find small photographs of people exercising and glue one action onto each whisker.

♦♦ **QUIET WHISKERS:** In addition to the "active whiskers" make a set of "quiet whiskers" (whisper a song, write your name in the air, sit on the floor, count your fingers, blink your eyes, open and shut your mouth, wiggle you nose). Play the same as you do with active whiskers.

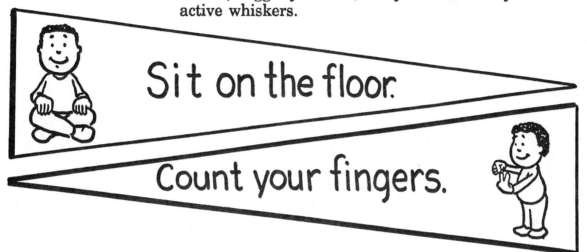

Sit on the floor.

Count your fingers.

♦♦♦ **HOP 5 TIMES:** Make the directions on each Whisker more specific. For example, "Hop 5 times" or "Crawl in a circle."

131

# ZOO DOMINOES

(Use Pattern Pages 241-246)

## YOU'LL NEED

2 pieces of colored posterboard
1 piece of white typing paper
Small pictures of 9 zoo animals which you can easily duplicate: tiger, lion,
    rhinoceros, giraffe, elephant, monkey, bear, camel, zebra
Permanent black marker
Clear Contact® paper/laminating if available
Resealable plastic bag

## TO MAKE ZOO DOMINOES

**Game Pieces**

1. Duplicate the zoo animal cards 8 times. Color the animals.

2. Cut out the cards so that you will have these pairs:

Elephant/giraffe, elephant/monkey, elephant/tiger, elephant/lion, elephant/rhinoceros, elephant/zebra, elephant/camel, elephant/bear

Giraffe/monkey, giraffe/tiger, giraffe/lion, giraffe/rhinoceros, giraffe/zebra, giraffe/camel, giraffe/bear

Monkey/tiger, monkey/lion, monkey/rhinoceros, monkey/zebra, monkey/camel, monkey/bear

Tiger/lion, tiger/rhinoceros, tiger/zebra, tiger/camel, tiger/bear

Lion/rhinoceros, lion/zebra, lion/camel, lion/bear

Rhinoceros/zebra, rhinoceros/camel, rhinoceros/bear

Zebra/camel, zebra/bear

Camel/bear

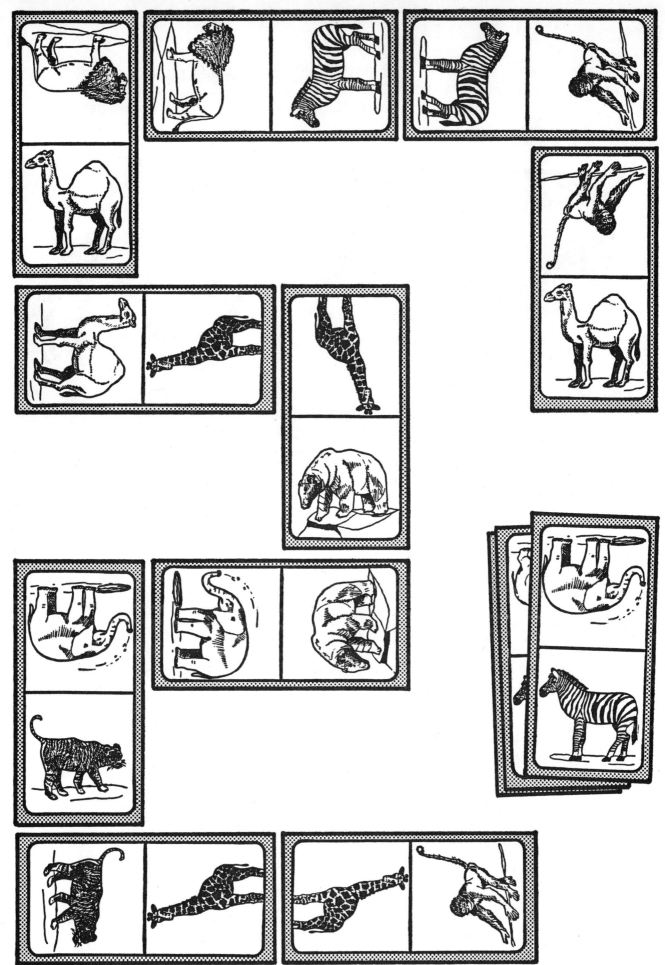

3. Cut 36, 3"x5½" rectangles from posterboard.

4. Glue the animal dominoes to the rectangles.

**Protect Your Game**

1. Laminate the game or cover both sides of each Zoo Animal Domino with clear Contact® paper.

2. Store them in a resealable plastic bag.

# TO PLAY <u>ZOO DOMINOES</u>

1. Put the first domino on the floor. Look at the 2 animals. Find a second domino which has one of the animals on it. Lay that domino next to the matching animal on the first domino.

2. Look at the animals again and find another matching one. Lay that domino next to the matching animal.

3. Continue matching the animals until all of the dominoes have been laid on the floor.

*While Playing Talk About*
~ Trips the players have taken to the zoo.
~ Noises the different animals make.
~ How the animals look.
~ Having a zoo animal for a pet.

# TO VARY YOUR GAME

♦ **EASY DOMINOES:** When constructing your dominoes use only 4-5 different zoo animals.

♦♦ **ZOO MATCH:** Instead of making dominoes, simply make sets of animal cards with a single zoo animal on each one and match the cards which are the same.

♦♦♦ **ANIMAL CONCENTRATION:** Instead of making dominoes, make 2 sets of matching cards with a single zoo animal on each one. Use them to play "Animal Concentration."

To play turn all of the zoo animal cards face down. The first player turns 2 cards over. If the animals are the same the player takes them and gets another turn. If not, the player turns the cards back over and the second player turns 2 cards over to see if he can make a match. The game continues until all of the zoo animals have been paired.

# OFF TO WORK

## YOU'LL NEED

1 piece of lightweight cardboard/tagboard
Drawn or magazine pictures of 10-12 people (about 5"-6" tall) who have different
    occupations, along with a picture of a hat and vehicle for each one
    (examples: firefighter, helmet, and fire truck; pilot, cap, and airplane; or a
    farmer, hat, and tractor)
3 feet of magnetic tape
Clear Contact® paper/laminating if available
Large resealable plastic bag

## TO MAKE OFF TO WORK

**Game Cards**

1. Cut 8, 3½"x8" rectangles from the lightweight cardboard. Duplicate, color, and glue one worker to each piece.

2. Cut 8, 3¼"x3¼" squares from the lightweight cardboard. Duplicate, color, and glue one hat on each piece.

3. Cut 8, 3½"x5" rectangles from the lightweight cardboard. Duplicate, color, and glue one vehicle on each piece.

136

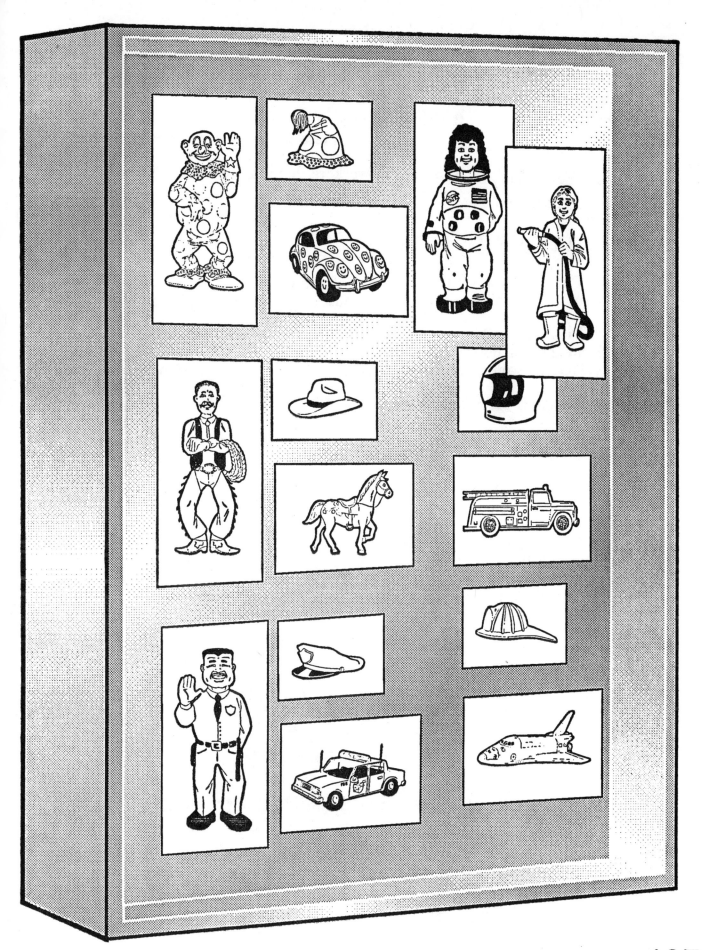

**Protect Your Game**

1. Laminate the game or cover both sides of each Worker, Hat, and Vehicle with clear Contact® paper.

2. Cut your piece of magnetic tape into 36, one inch pieces. Glue one piece to the back of each game card.

3. Store the workers, hats, and vehicles in the resealable bag.

# TO PLAY <u>OFF TO WORK</u>

1. Put all of the workers together at the top of a large magnetic board. Group the vehicles and hats and put them near the top also.

2. Pick one worker and put him near the bottom of the magnetic board. Find the hat he would wear to work and put it next to him. Find the vehicle he would drive and put it next to the worker and below the hat.

3. Choose a second worker and match him with his hat and vehicle.

4. Continue in this manner until all of the workers are 'off to work' for the day.

*While Playing Talk About*
- What jobs the players do at home.
- What the different workers do at their jobs.
- What tools the workers use at their jobs.
- People the players know who go to work and what they do at work.
- People the players know who do jobs which are pictured in the game.

# TO VARY YOUR GAME

♦ **VEHICLE MATCH:** When constructing your game, use workers who have their hats on. To play, match the workers with their vehicles.

♦♦♦ **WORKER GO FISH:** Use the worker cards to play a variation of "Go Fish." To construct the game, duplicate the worker cards several times. (Make sure that there is an even number of each occupation.) Back each one with lightweight cardboard and laminate them.

   To play, deal 3 or 4 cards to the players and put the rest of the cards face down in the middle. The players then look at their cards to find pairs, and lay them down if they have any. Then the first player chooses one of his unmatched cards and asks another player, "Do you have any _____?" If that player has one, he gives it to the first player. The first player then makes a match, and lays down the pair. If the player doesn't have the card, he says, "Go fish." The first player then picks a card from the middle pile. Continue until all of the cards have been matched.

# CLOWNING AROUND

(Use Pattern Pages 247-254)

## YOU'LL NEED

1 piece of light colored posterboard
10 different colored 3"x6" pieces of posterboard
Permanent black marker
Set of colored markers
Lightweight cardboard/tagboard
Clear Contact® paper/laminating if available

## TO MAKE CLOWNING AROUND

**Game Board**

1. Using the black marker, draw a large, simply shaped clown wearing a full-fitting suit on the light colored posterboard.

2. Take a 2½" circular shape or template, and draw 10 circles on each side of the clown's suit.

**Game Pieces**

1. Trace 2, 2½" polka dots on each 3"x6" piece of posterboard.

2. Cut out the 20 polka-dots.

**Storage Pocket**

1. Cut a 3"x7" rectangle from the lightweight cardboard. Round the corners to look like a pocket. Add details.

2. Drizzle glue along the 2 sides and bottom edge of the pocket and fasten it to the back of the clown.

**Protect Your Game**

1. Laminate the game or cover both sides of the Clown and his Polka-Dots with clear Contact® paper.

2. Carefully slit open the top edge of the pocket.

3. Store the clown's polka-dots in it.

140

141

# TO PLAY <u>CLOWNING AROUND</u>

1. Lay the clown's polka dots near his feet.

2. Choose one dot. Find the matching one.

3. Place one polka-dot on one side of the clown's suit and the matching dot on the other side.

4. The second player chooses a polka-dot, finds its mate, and lays one on each side of the clown's suit.

5. Continue letting each player pair the polka-dots and place them on the clown.

### *While Playing Talk About*
~ The colors of the clown's polka-dots.
~ Times the players have seen clowns.
~ Tricks that clowns do.
~ Reasons why clowns are funny.

# TO VARY YOUR GAME

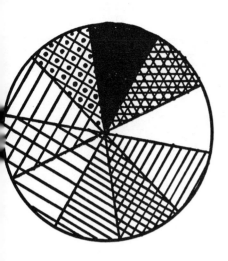

♦ **NAME THE COLORS:** When playing the game, have each player in turn choose a polka-dot, name its color if he can, and place it on the clown's suit. Continue until all of the dots are on the suit.

♦♦ **SPIN A COLOR:** When constructing the game, in addition to the clown and his pairs of polka-dots, make a color wheel with 10 equal sections. Color the sections to match the polka dots. Add a spinner.

To play, have the first player flick the spinner, name the color, find a matching polka-dot, and place it on the clown's suit. Continue until all of the polka-dots are on the clown's suit.

♦♦♦ **MATCH THE NUMBERS:** After you have laminated your game, use a permanent black marker to write a numeral on each circle on the clown's suit and corresponding numerals on each of the polka-dots.

To play, have the players match the numerals on the clown's suit with his polka dots. (When finished with this variation, wipe the numerals off by gently rubbing a little fingernail polish remover on each one. Wipe clean and you are ready to use the clown again.)

# PATTERNS

# SUPPLIES AND MATERIALS LIST

## SUPPLIES

All colors of crayons
All colors of markers
Fabric glue
Paper punch
Ruler
Scissors

Spray glue
Straight pins
White glue
X-Acto knife
Yardstick

## MATERIALS

2lb and 3lb metal coffee cans with lids
3/4" round self-adhesive colored dots
11/4" round self-adhesive colored dots
1" round smiley self-adhesive dots
All colors of construction paper
All colors of posterboard
Black and white felt
Clear Contact® Paper/laminating if available
Colored file folders
Large piece of corrugated cardboard
Lightweight cardboard/tagboard
Magnetic tape
Metal brads
Metal rings
Pocket folders
Popsicle sticks/tongue depressors
Resealable plastic bags
Sandpaper
Slightly patterned Contact® paper
White and pink large index cards
White duplicating paper
Yellow shelf paper/butcher paper

# OFF TO SCHOOL

# OFF TO SCHOOL

# OFF TO SCHOOL

# OFF TO SCHOOL

# IN THE APPLE TREE

# SHAPE MATCH

# SHAPE MATCH

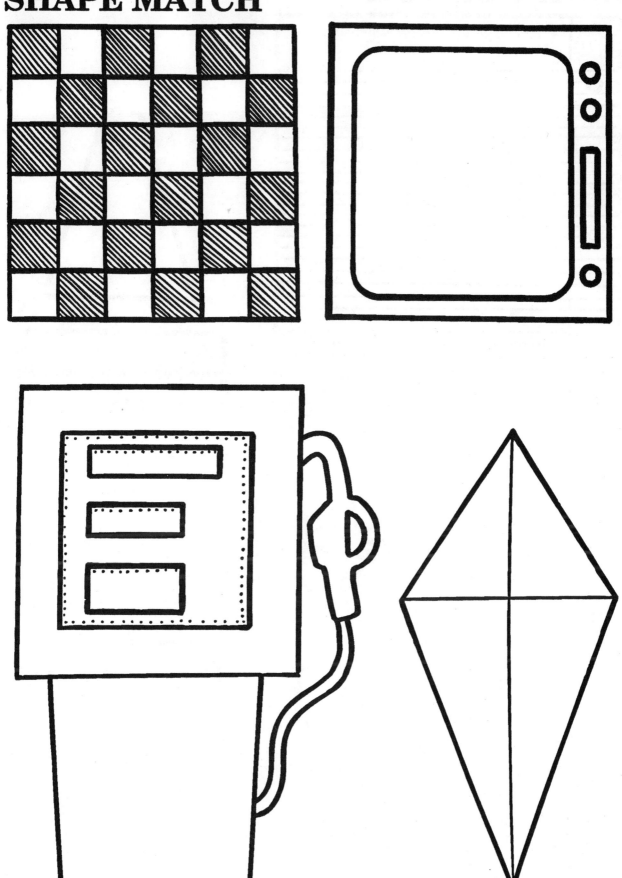

# SHAPE MATCH

# SHAPE MATCH

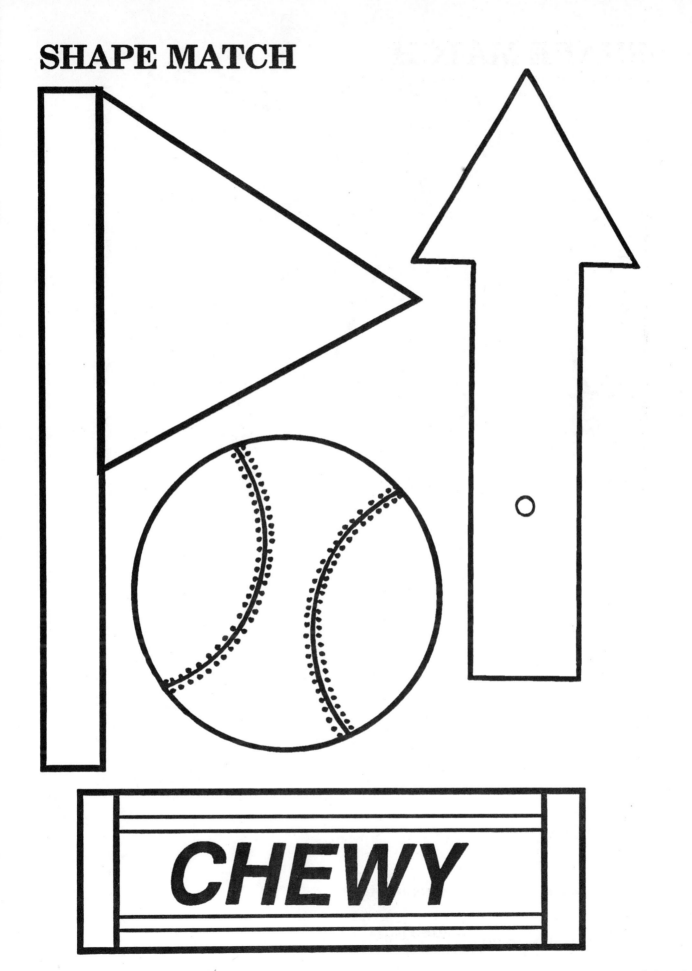

CHEWY

# SHAPE MATCH

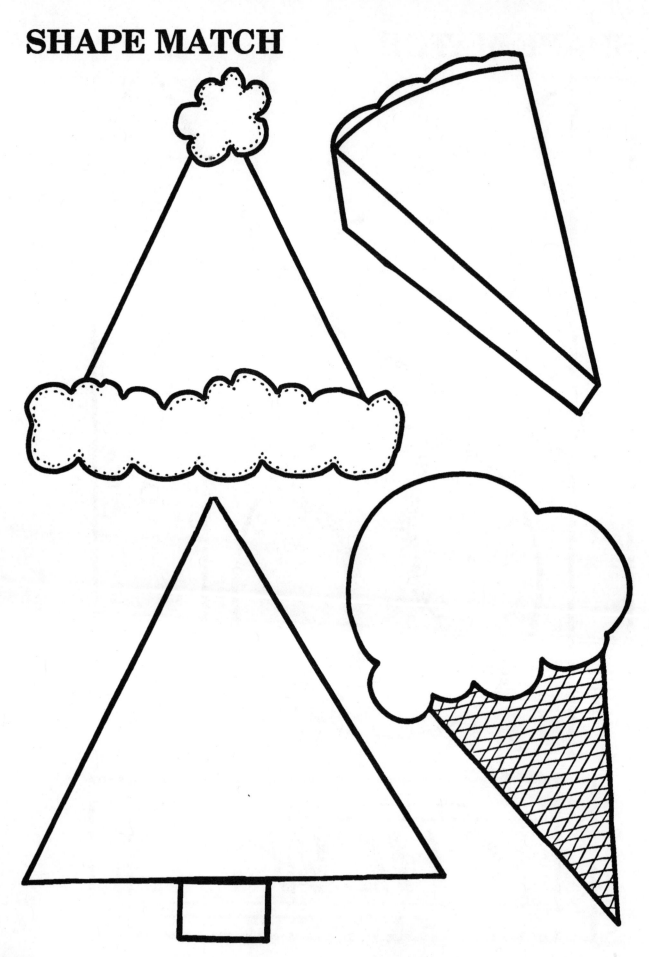

# SHAPE MATCH

# SHAPE MATCH

# SHAPE MATCH

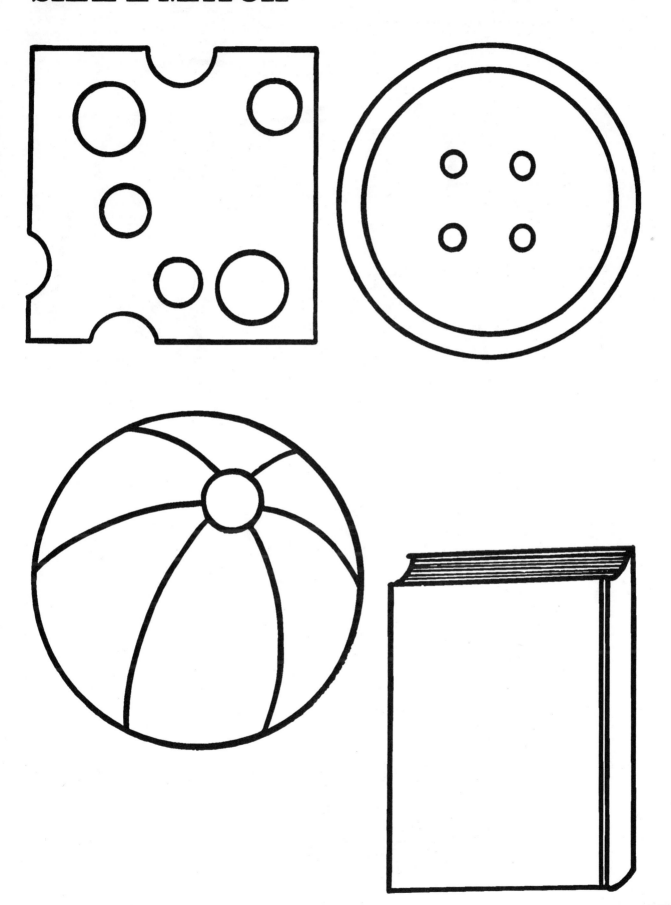

# WALK AROUND THE ZOO

# WALK AROUND THE ZOO

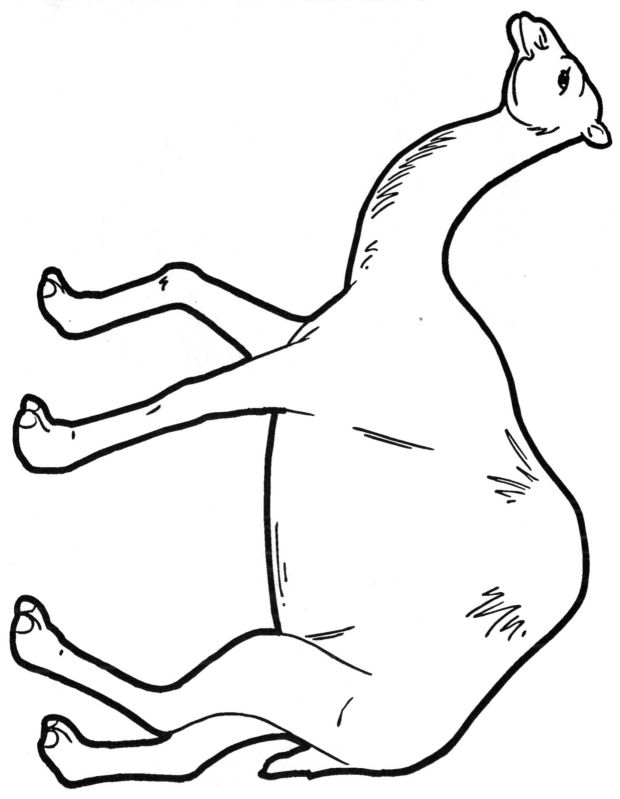

# WALK AROUND THE ZOO

# WALK AROUND THE ZOO

# WALK AROUND THE ZOO

# WALK AROUND THE ZOO

# WALK AROUND THE ZOO

# CLIP IT

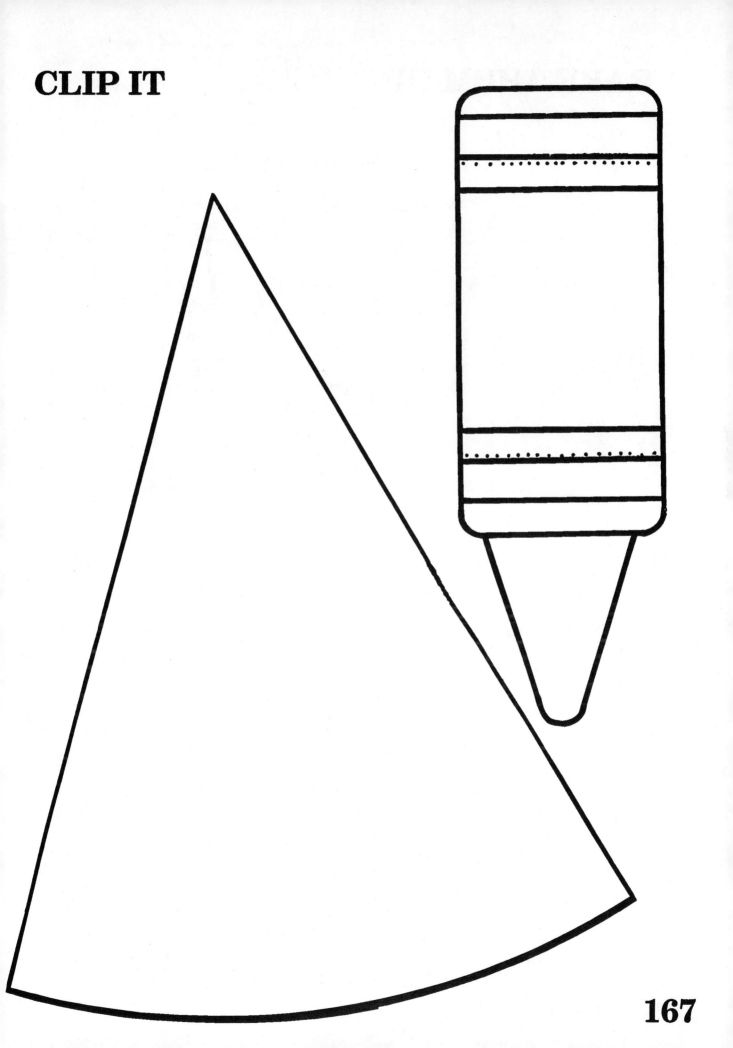

# RAKE THEM UP

# RAKE THEM UP

# RAKE THEM UP

# RAKE THEM UP

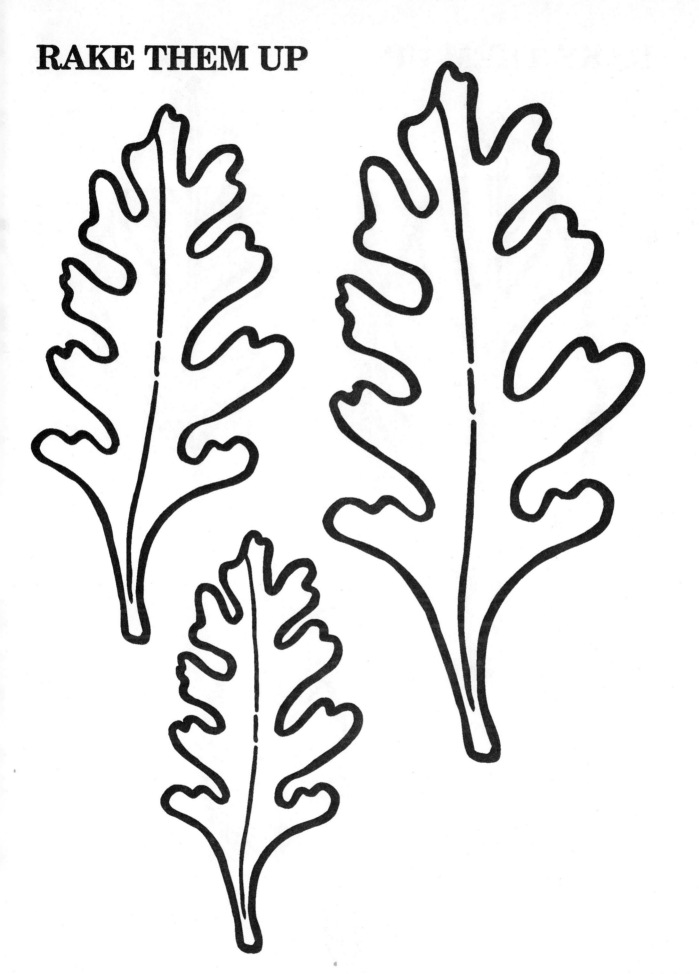

# RAKE THEM UP

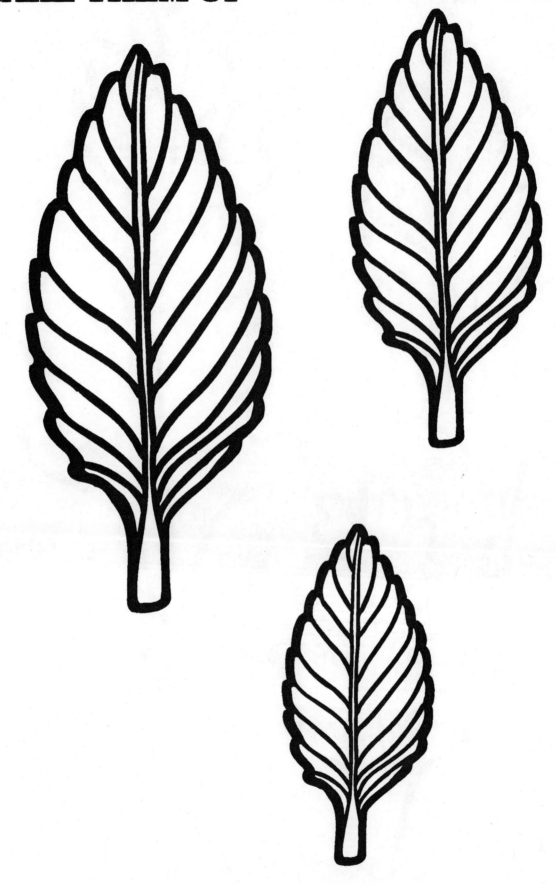

# RAKE THEM UP

# RAKE THEM UP

# ALPHABET CRASH

Garage

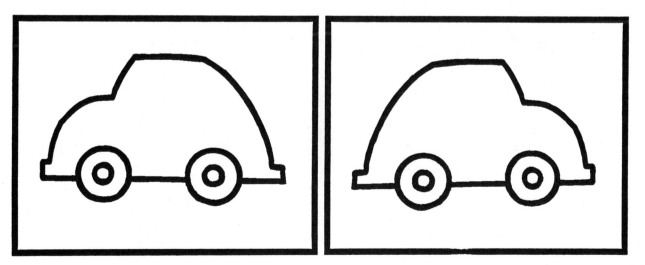

# ALPHABET CRASH

# DRESS FROSTY

# DRESS FROSTY

# PETER PANDA

# PETER PANDA

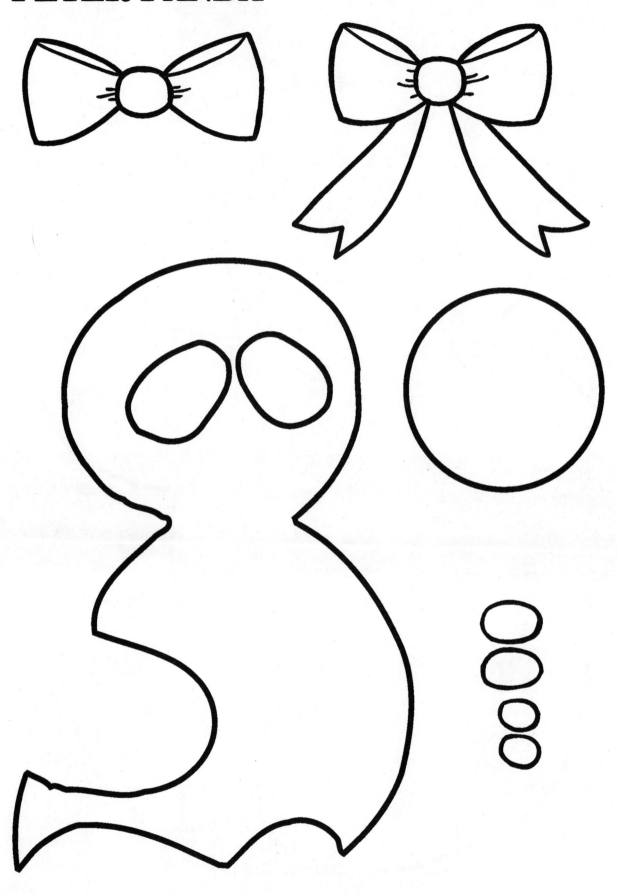

# SAMMY SHAPE

MAKE TWO

MAKE ONE

# SAMMY SHAPE

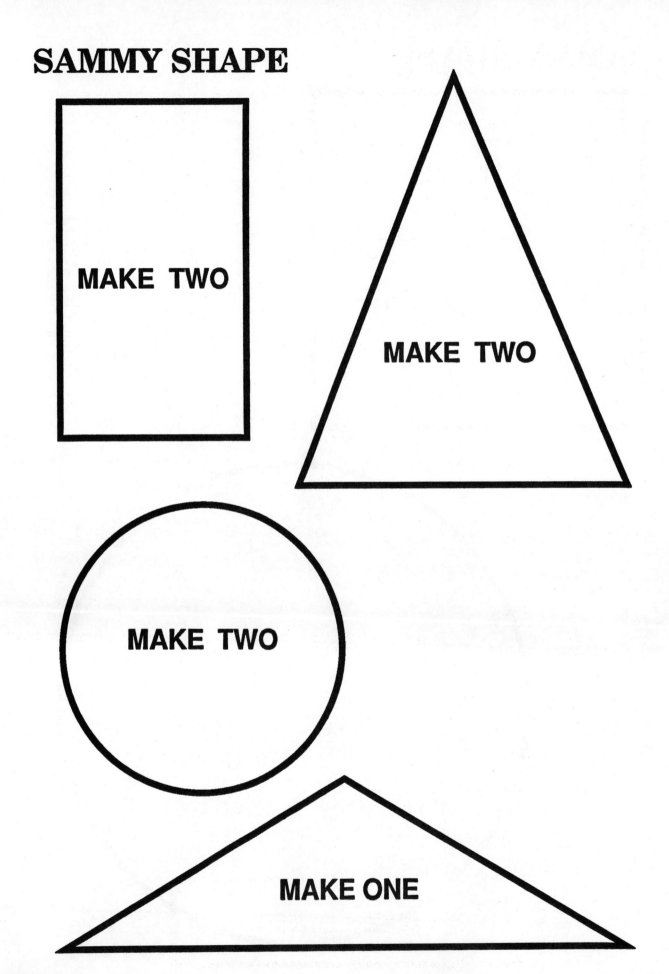

MAKE TWO

MAKE TWO

MAKE TWO

MAKE ONE

# SAMMY SHAPE

MAKE ONE

MAKE ONE

MAKE TWO

MAKE ONE

# ALPHABET SOUP

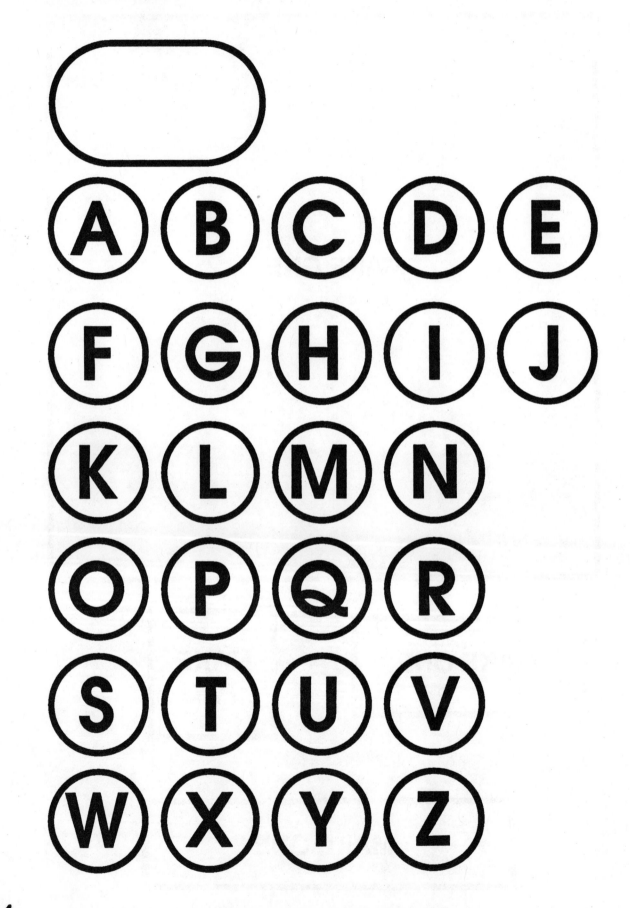

# ALPHABET SOUP

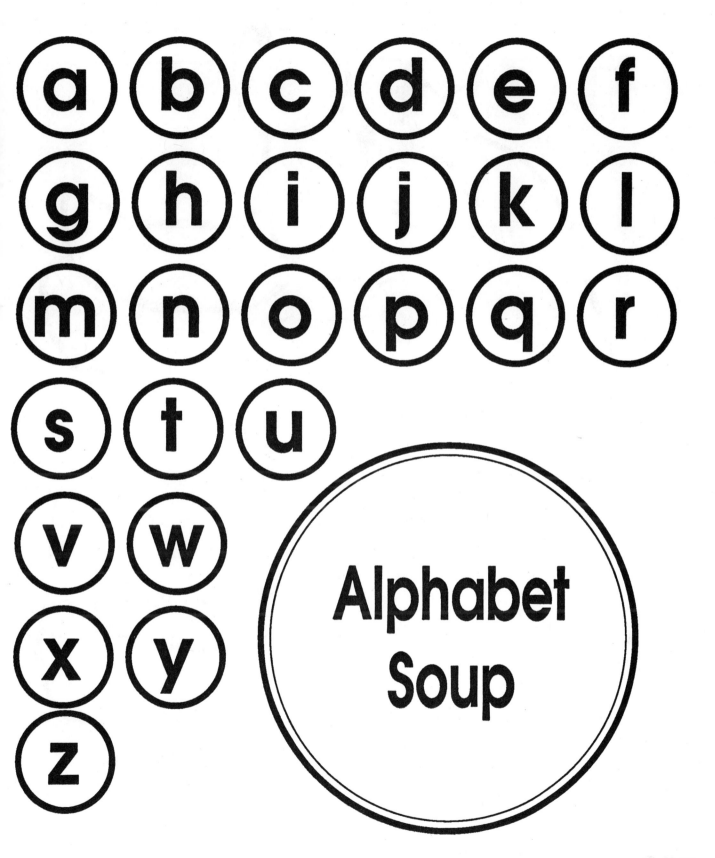

# GREGORY GROUNDHOG

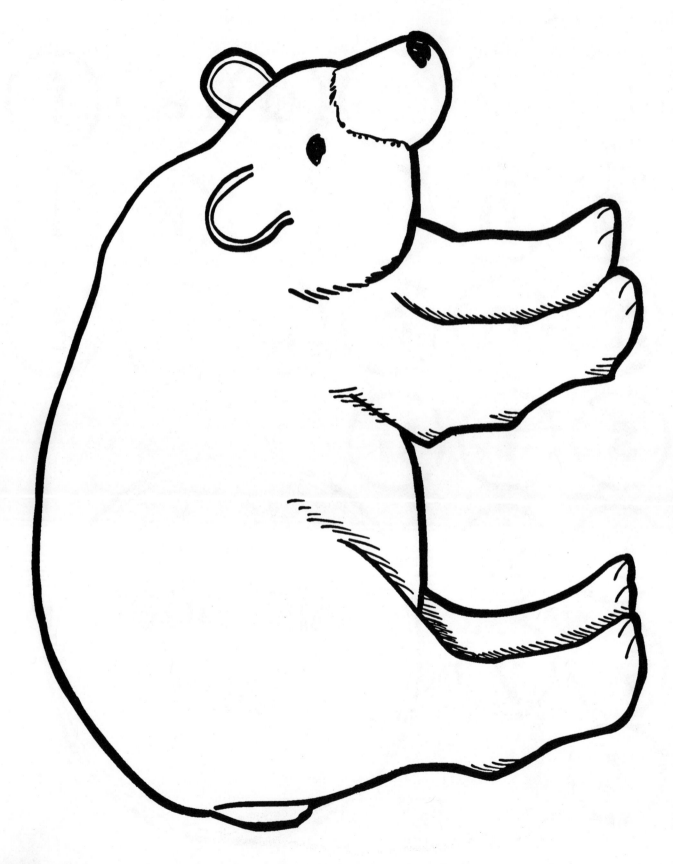

# GREGORY GROUNDHOG

# GREGORY GROUNDHOG

188

# GREGORY GROUNDHOG

# GREGORY GROUNDHOG

# GREGORY GROUNDHOG

Mitten Match

# MITTEN MATCH

# FOOD TRAIN

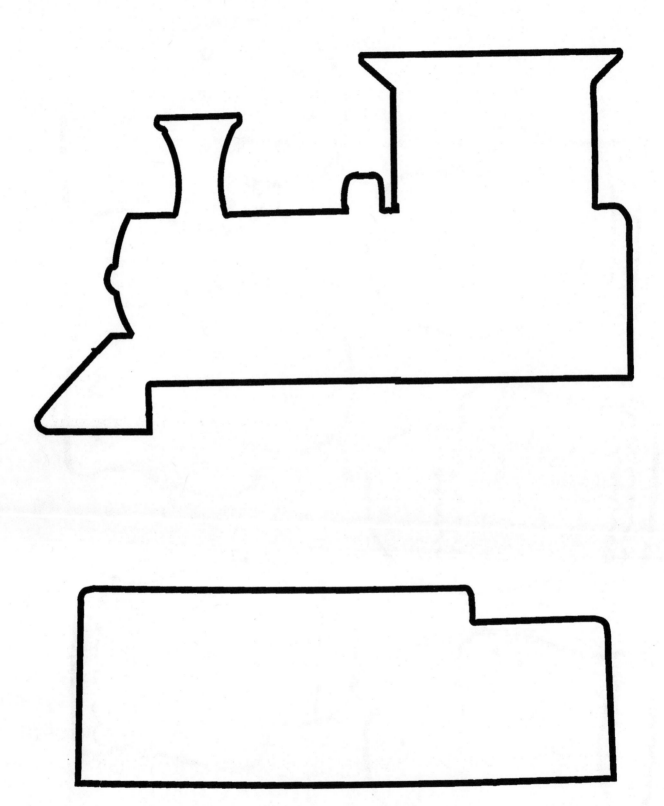

# FOOD TRAIN

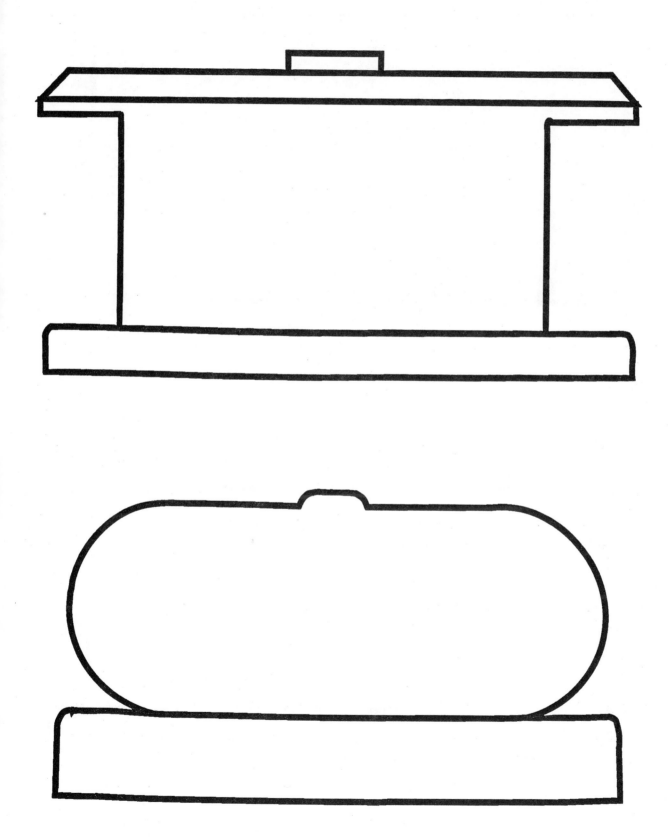

# FOOD TRAIN

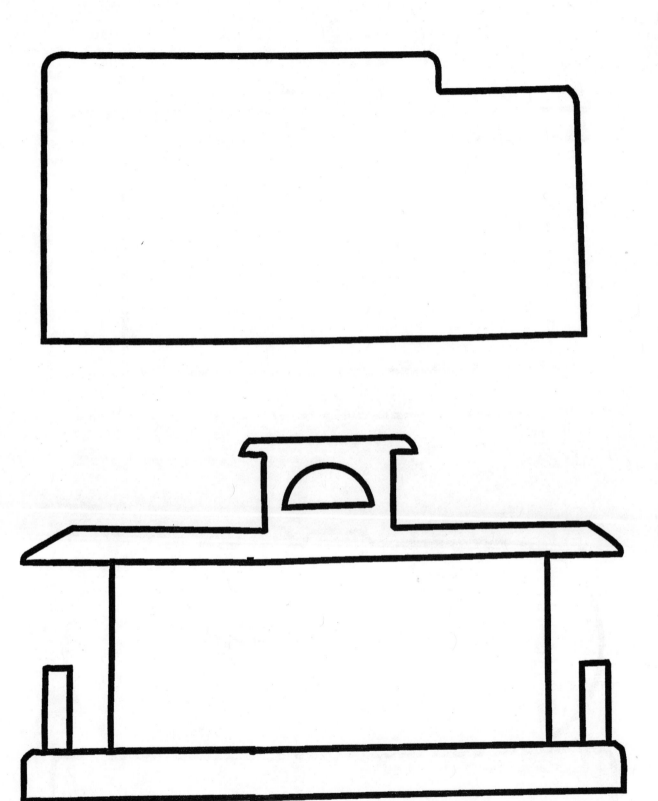

# FOOD TRAIN

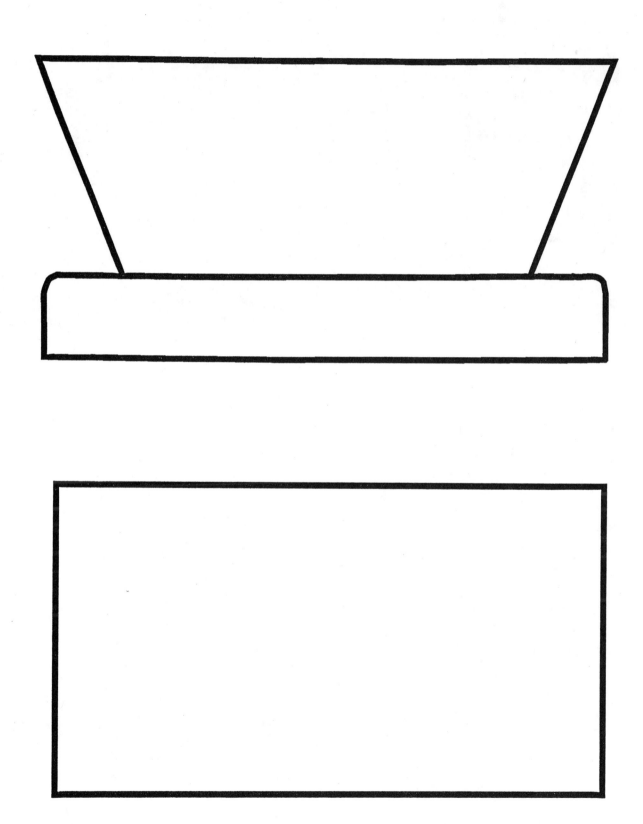

# FOOD TRAIN

## DAIRY

# FOOD TRAIN

## SWEETS

# FOOD TRAIN
## GRAINS

# FOOD TRAIN

## MEATS

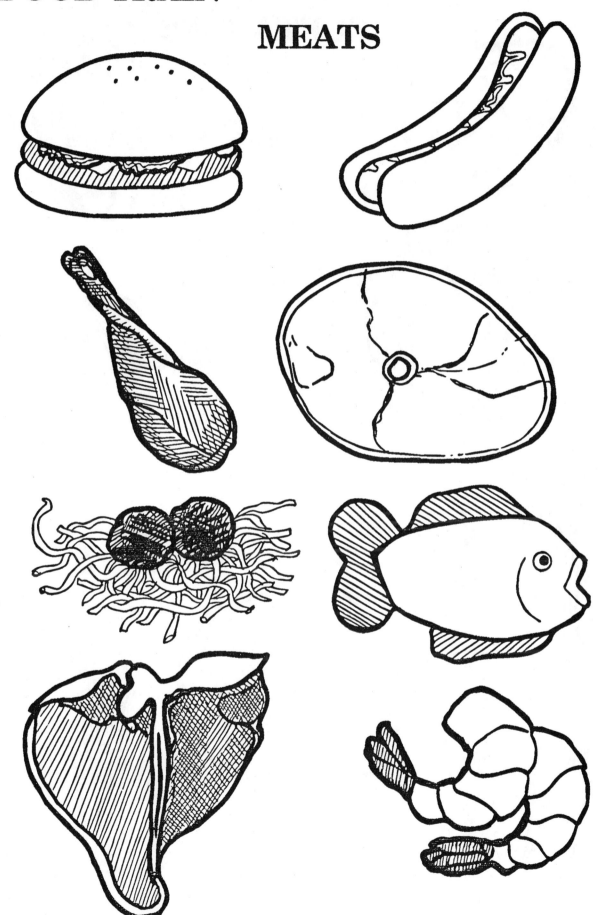

# FOOD TRAIN

## VEGETABLES

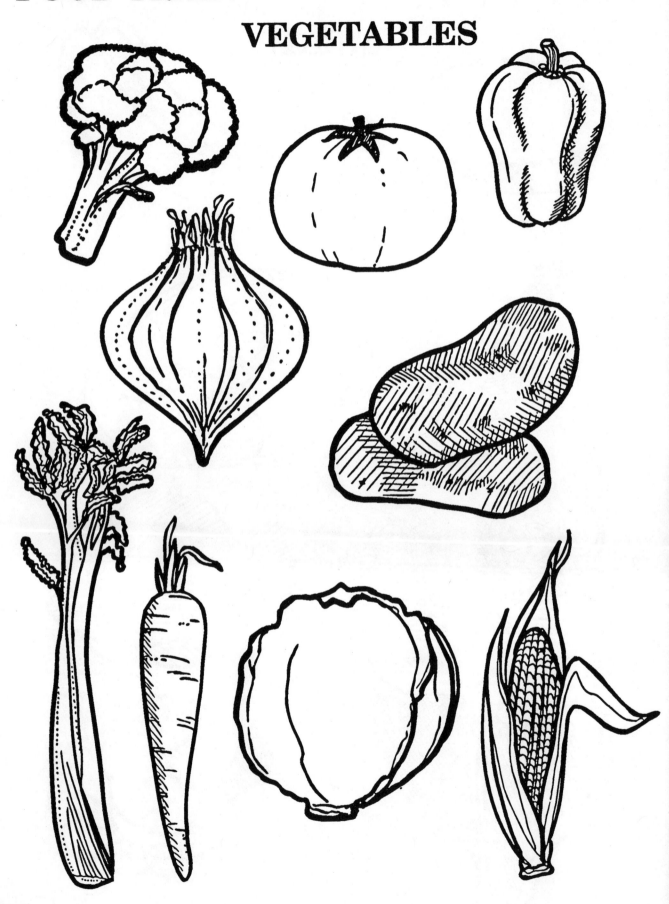

# FOOD TRAIN

## FRUITS

# RAINDROP SPLASH

# RAINDROP SPLASH

# RAINDROP SPLASH

# GERI GIRAFFE

# MINI DINO JUMP

# MINI DINO JUMP

# MINI DINO JUMP

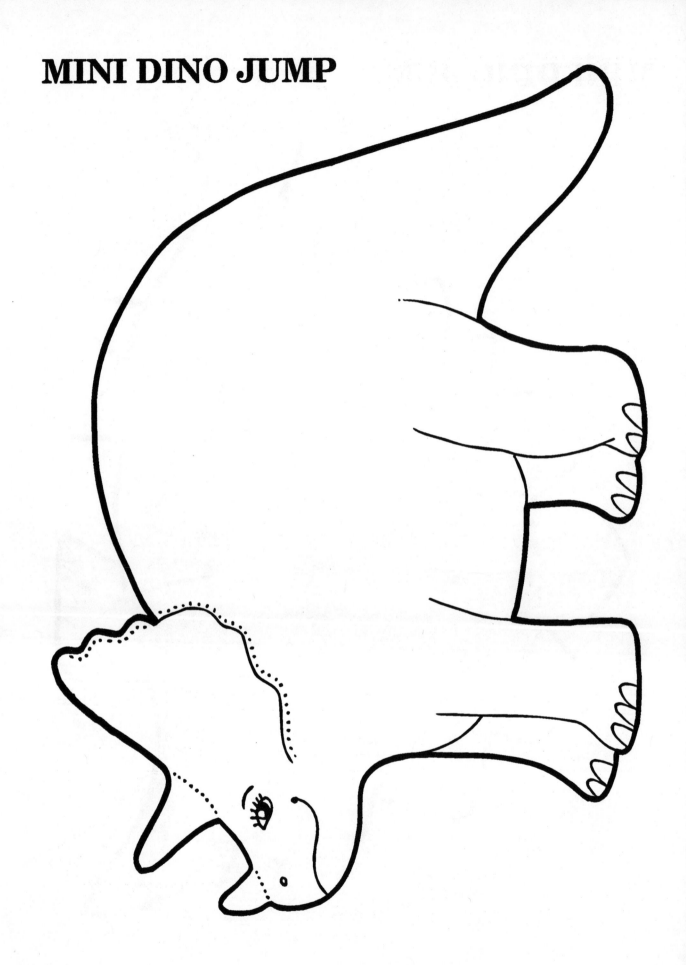

# MINI DINO JUMP

# COPY CAT

# COPY CAT

# COLOR BINGO

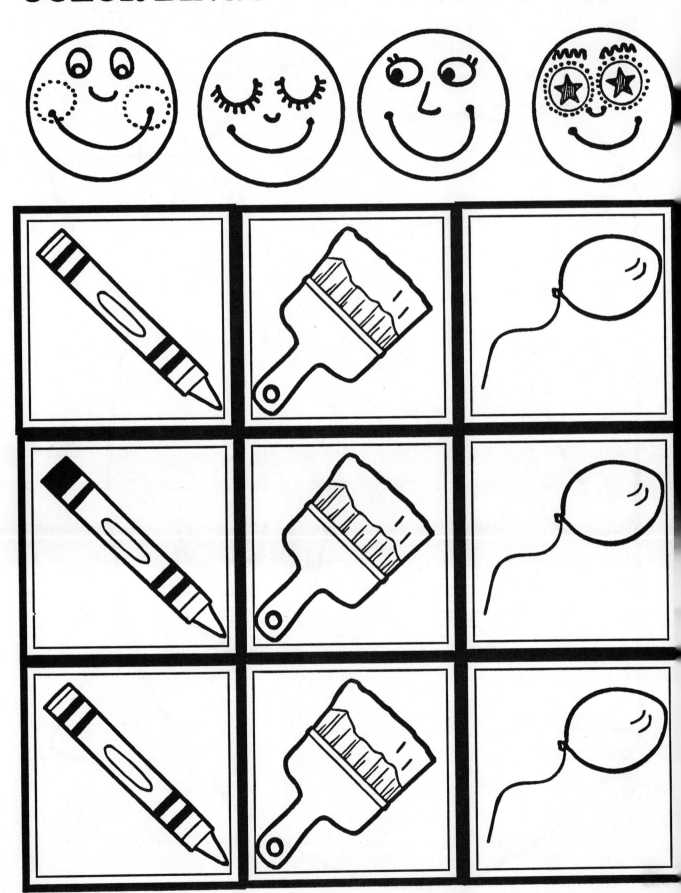

# LACING NUMBERS

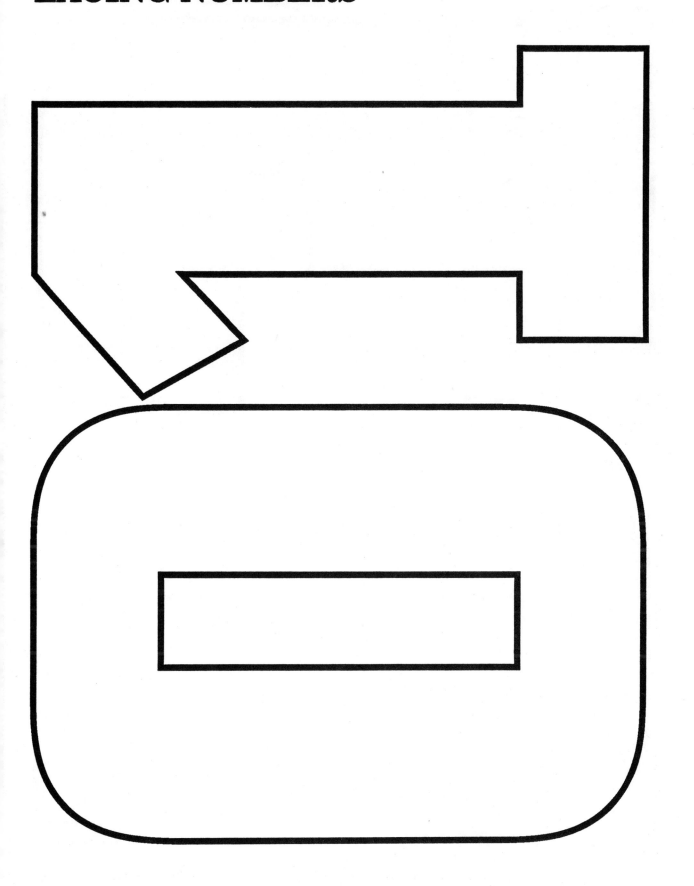

# LACING NUMBERS

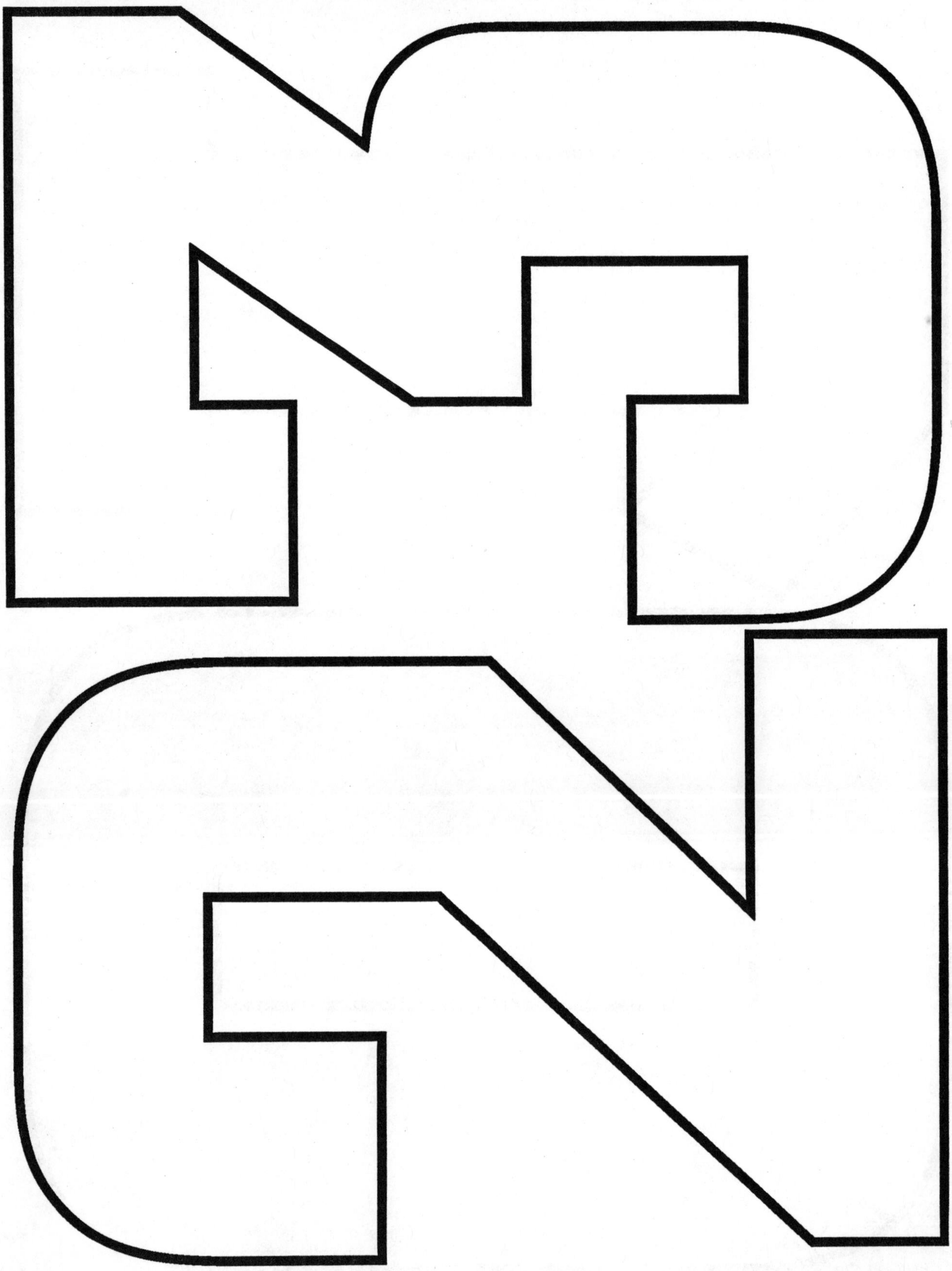

# LACING NUMBERS

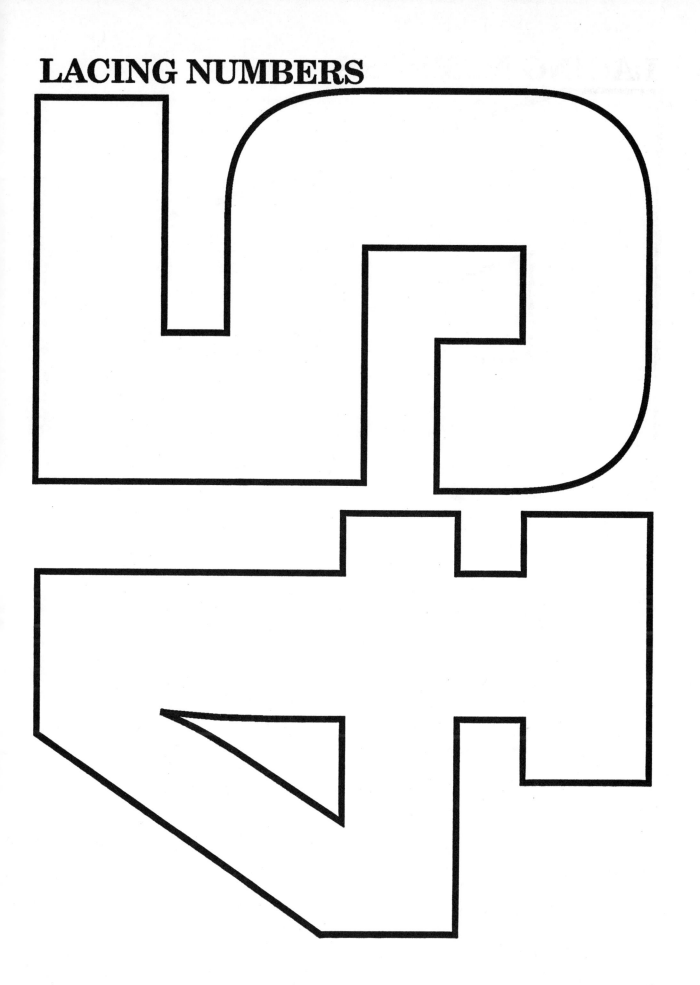

# LACING NUMBERS

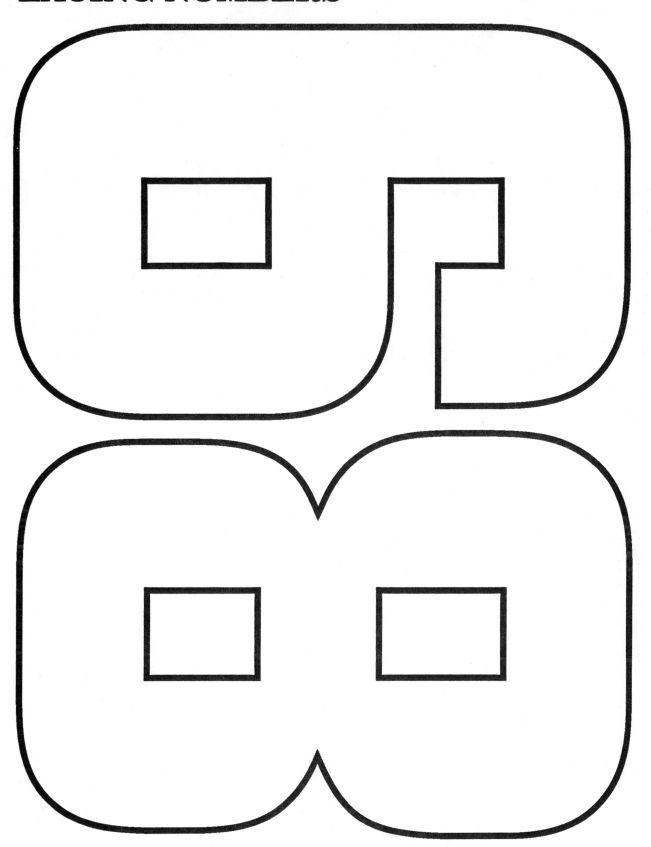

Farm

Beach

City

# Misc. Cards

# I SPY

## Beach Cards

# I SPY

## Farm Cards

# I SPY

## City Cards

# IN THE BARN

# IN THE BARN

# FAVORITE FLAVORS

# HAPPY BIRTHDAY

# HAPPY BIRTHDAY

# HAPPY BIRTHDAY

# HAPPY BIRTHDAY

# HAPPY BIRTHDAY

# 1, 2, 3 LADYBUG

# FEELINGS CONCENTRATION

# FEELINGS CONCENTRATION

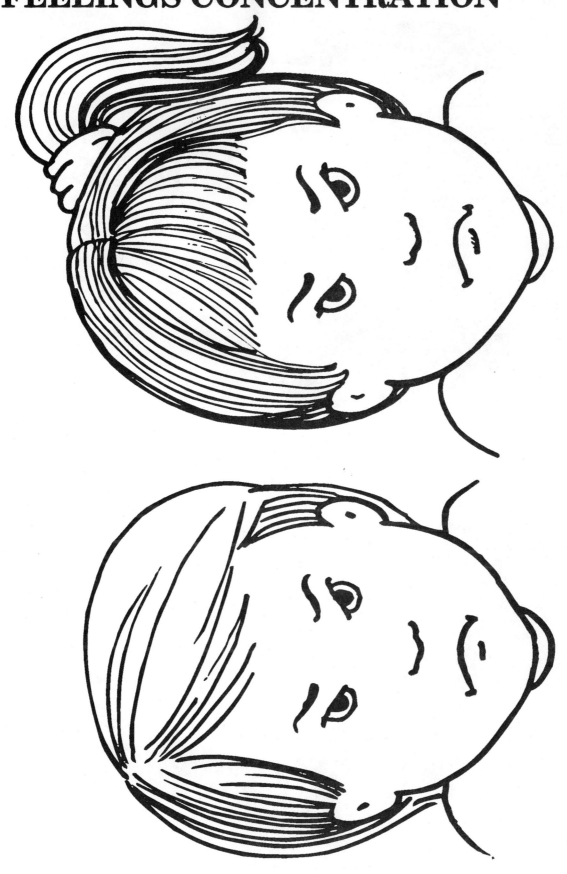

# FEELINGS CONCENTRATION

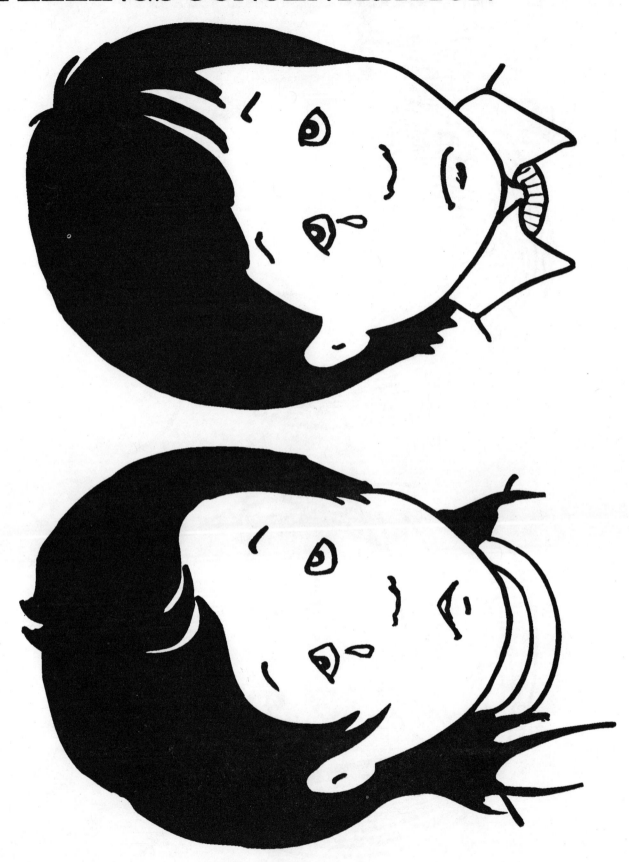

# FEELINGS CONCENTRATION

# FEELINGS CONCENTRATION

# WHISKERS SAYS

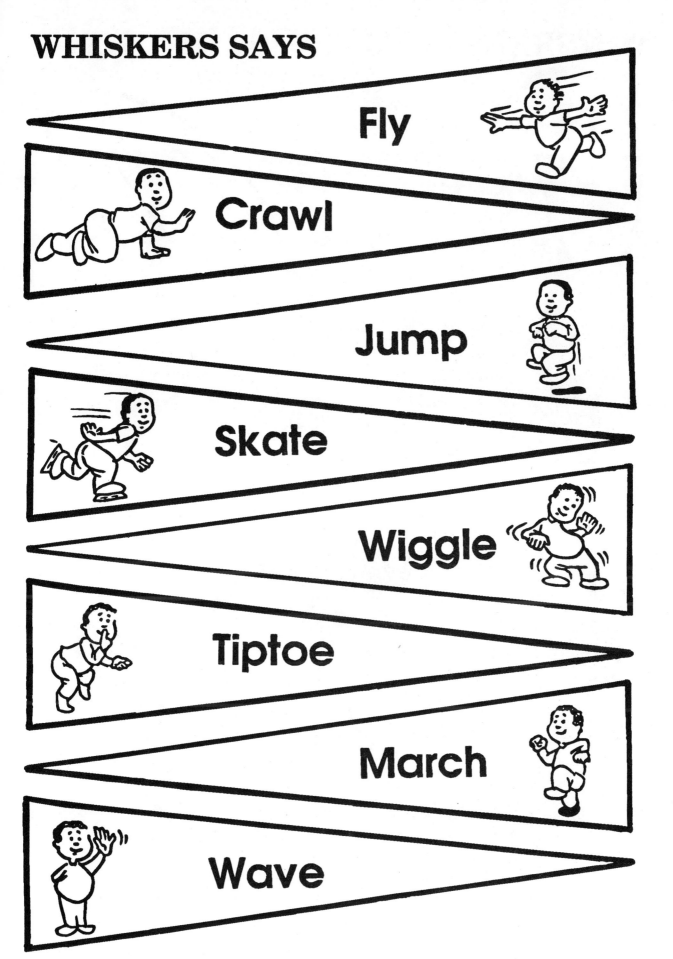

Fly

Crawl

Jump

Skate

Wiggle

Tiptoe

March

Wave

# WHISKERS SAYS

# ZOO DOMINOES

# ZOO DOMINOES

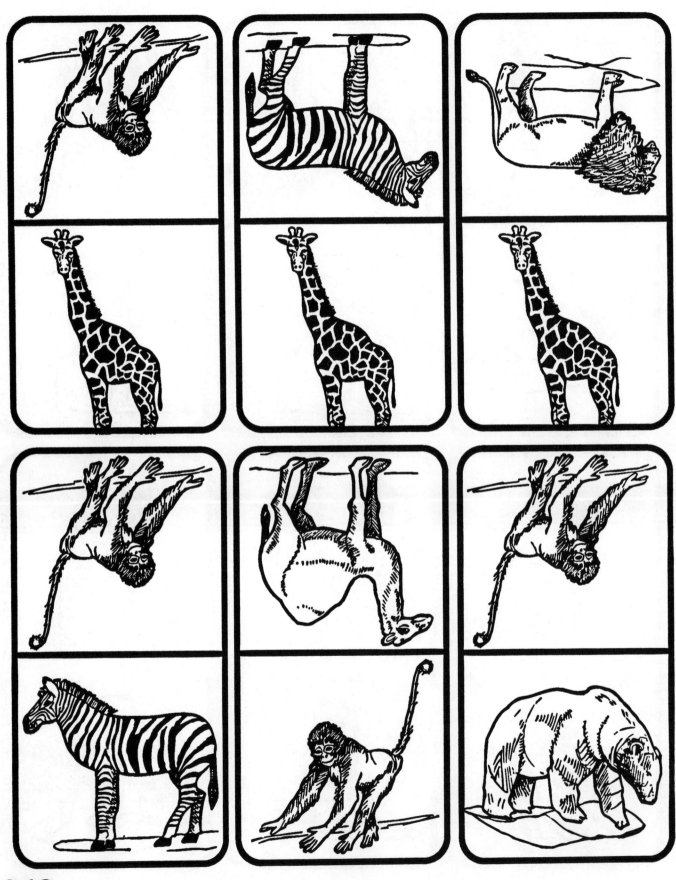

# ZOO DOMINOES

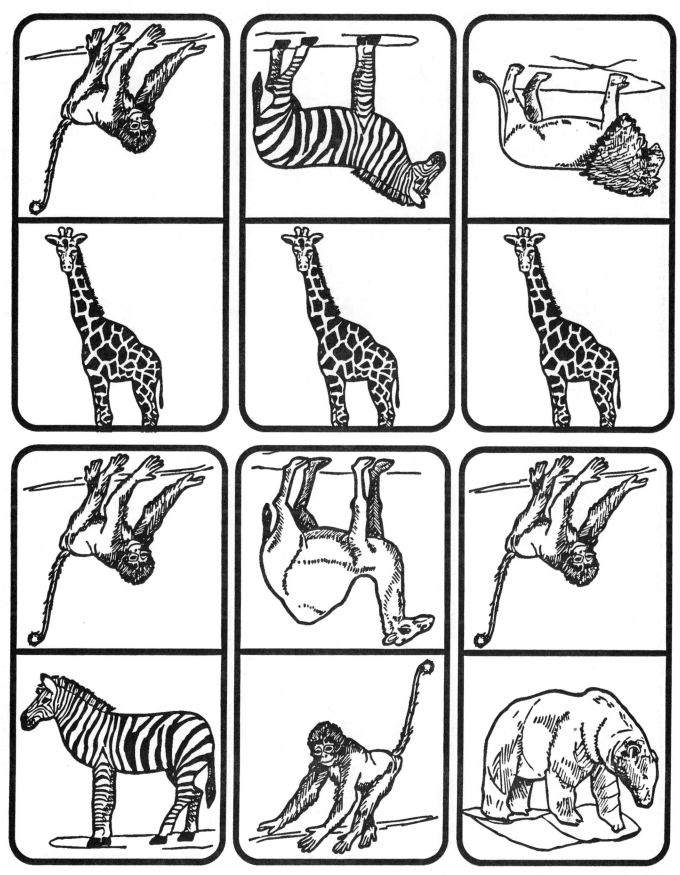

# ZOO DOMINOES

# ZOO DOMINOES

# ZOO DOMINOES

# OFF TO WORK

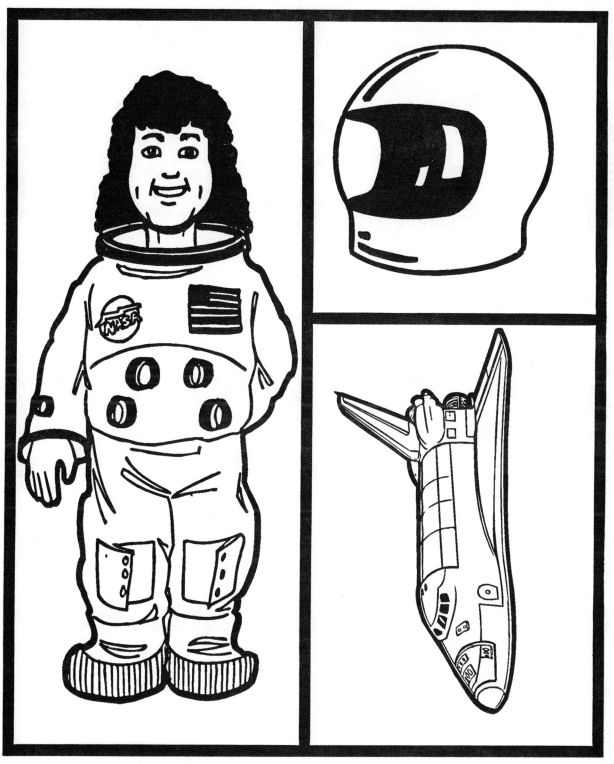

# OFF TO WORK

# OFF TO WORK

# OFF TO WORK

# OFF TO WORK

# OFF TO WORK

# OFF TO WORK

# OFF TO WORK

# FOR EVERY MONTH

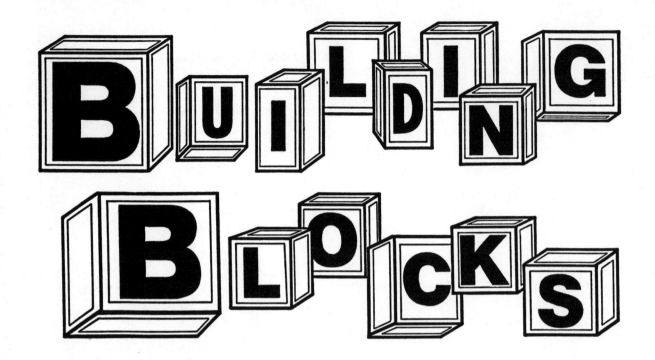

**BUILDING BLOCKS**

*an activity newspaper for adults*
*and their young children*

**TAKE
A LOOK
AT
BUILDING
BLOCKS
NEWSPAPER**

**PUBLISHED:**
10 times a year
including an expanded
summer issue.

**RATES:**
1 Year ~ $20⁰⁰
2 Years ~ $36⁵⁰
3 Years ~ $50⁰⁰
Sample ~ $ 3⁰⁰

SEND YOUR NAME, ADDRESS
(INCLUDING ZIP CODE), AND
PAYMENT TO:

**BUILDING BLOCKS**
38W567 Brindlewood
Elgin, Il   60123

BUILDING BLOCKS is a 20 page early childhood activity newspaper offering a total curriculum resource to use in your classroom and share with your parents.

**MONTHLY FEATURES** include:

~ Reproducible parent activity calendar.

~ Activity pages highlighting language, art, physical, science/math, creative, and self/social activities which are easy to plan and implement.

~ Ready-to-use charts, games, and/or posters.

~ Special activity page for toddlers and twos.

~ Large easy-to-use illustrations.

~ 4 page **FEATURED TOPIC** *Pull-Out Section.*

# Library

## The Circle Time Series

*by Liz and Dick Wilmes.* Hundreds of activities for large and small groups of children. Each book is filled with Language and Active games, Fingerplays, Songs, Stories, Snacks, and more. A great resource for every library shelf.

### Circle Time Book
Captures the spirit of 39 holidays and seasons.
ISBN 0-943452-00-7                                    $ 9.95

### Everyday Circle Times
Over 900 ideas. Choose from 48 topics divided into 7 sections: self-concept, basic concepts, animals, foods, science, occupations, and recreation.
ISBN 0-943452-01-5                                    $14.95

### More Everyday Circle Times
Divided into the same 7 sections as EVERYDAY. Features new topics such as Birds and Pizza, plus all new ideas for some familiar topics contained in EVERYDAY.
ISBN 0-943452-14-7                                    $14.95

### Yearful of Circle Times
52 different topics to use weekly, by seasons, or mixed throughout the year. New Friends, Signs of Fall, Snowfolk Fun, and much more.
ISBN 0-943452-10-4                                    $14.95

## Paint Without Brushes

*by Liz and Dick Wilmes.* Use common materials which you already have to discover the painting possibilities in your classroom! PAINT WITHOUT BRUSHES gives your children open-ended art activities to explore paint in lots of creative ways. A valuable art resource. One you'll want to use daily.
ISBN 0-943452-15-5                                    $12.95

## Gifts, Cards, and Wraps

*by Wilmes and Zavodsky.* Help the children sparkle with the excitement of gift giving. Filled with thoughtful gifts, unique wraps, and special cards which the children can make and give. They're sure to bring smiles.
ISBN 0-943452-06-6                                    $ 7.95

## Everyday Bulletin Boards

*by Wilmes and Moehling.* Features borders, murals, backgrounds, and other open-ended art to display on your bulletin boards. Plus board ideas with patterns, which teachers can make and use to enhance their curriculum.
ISBN 0-943452-09-0                                    $ 8.95

## Exploring Art

*by Liz and Dick Wilmes.* EXPLORING ART is divided by months. Over 250 art ideas for paint, chalk, doughs, scissors, and more. Easy to set-up in your classroom.
ISBN 0-943452-05-8                                    $16.95

CIRCLE TIME

ART

# Parachute Play

*by Liz and Dick Wilmes.* A year 'round approach to one of the most versatile pieces of large muscle equipment. Starting with basic techniques, PARACHUTE PLAY provides over 100 activities to use with your parachute.
**ISBN 0-943452-03-1**      **$ 7.95**

# Classroom Parties

*by Susan Spaete.* Each party plan suggests decorations, trimmings, and snacks which the children can easily make to set a festive mood. Choose from games, songs, art activities, stories, and related experiences which will add to the spirit and fun.
**ISBN 0-943452-07-4**      **$ 8.95**

# Imagination Stretchers

*by Liz and Dick Wilmes.* Perfect for whole language. Over 400 conversation starters for creative discussions, simple lists, and beginning dictation and writing.
**ISBN 0-943452-04-X**      **$ 6.95**

# Parent Programs and Open Houses

*by Susan Spaete.* Filled with a wide variety of year 'round presentations, pre-registration ideas, open houses, and end-of-the-year gatherings. All involve the children from the planning stages through the programs.
**ISBN 0-943452-08-2**      **$ 9.95**

# Learning Centers

*by Liz and Dick Wilmes.* Hundreds of open-ended activities to quickly involve and excite your children. You'll use it every time you plan and whenever you need a quick, additional activity. A must for every teacher's bookshelf.
**ISBN 0-943452-13-9**      **$16.95**

# Felt Board Fun

*by Liz and Dick Wilmes.* Make your felt board come alive. Discover how versatile it is as the children become involved with a wide range of activities. This unique book has over 150 ideas with accompanying patterns.
**ISBN 0-943452-02-3**      **$14.95**

# Table & Floor Games

*by Liz and Dick Wilmes.* 32 easy-to-make, fun-to-play table games with accompanying patterns. Teach beginning concepts such as matching, counting, colors, alphabet recognition, sorting, and so on. Over 100 pages of patterns (foods, animals, transportation, feelings, nature, etc.) ready to trace or photocopy. Within a short time you'll have a variety of games to play with your children. You can also use patterns for felt board stories, bulletin boards, quick note paper, charts, newsletters, and children's dictations.
**ISBN 0-943452-16-3**      **$16.95**

**A**ll books available from
teacher bookstores,
school supply catalogs
or directly from:

**38W567 Brindlewood, Elgin, Illinois 60123**
**708-742-1013   800-233-2448   708-742-1054 (FAX)**

*Thank you for your order.*